GW00697121

This book belongs to:

Name   Dawn & Male Roberts

Address: 4 Goldbank,

Nanstallon,

BODMIN

Cornwall.

PL30 5UA

Telephone: 01208 831208

Bought September 1999.

For Joanne and Jack,
without whose love and encouragement
this book could not have been produced

A LOG BOOK OF THE MOUNTAINS OF ENGLAND

Mark Woosey

Copyright © Mark Woosey, 1995

All Rights Reserved. No part of this publication may be reproduced, stored in a retrieval system, or transmitted in any form or by any means – electronic, mechanical, photocopying, recording, or otherwise – without prior written permission from the publisher.

Published by Sigma Leisure – an imprint of
Sigma Press, 1 South Oak Lane, Wilmslow, Cheshire SK9 6AR, England.

British Library Cataloguing in Publication Data
A CIP record for this book is available from the British Library.

ISBN: 1-85058-394-3

Typesetting and Design by: Sigma Press, Wilmslow, Cheshire.

Cover: Ascending Blencathra via Sharp Edge *(photograph by G. Beech)*

Printed by: J.W. Arrowsmith Ltd, Bristol

Disclaimer: the information in this book is given in good faith and is believed to be correct at the time of publication. No responsibility is accepted by either the author or publisher for errors or omissions, or for any loss or injury howsoever caused. Only you can judge your own fitness, competence and experience.

Preface

My introduction to mountains was as a teenager. My father was contracted to extend the Belsfield Hotel in Bowness on Windermere and consequently I made my first visits to the Lake District. I remember very little about that period and was probably more interested in the hotel than the vistas from it.

Later, I worked on producing maps of Great Langdale and the profile of Mickleden Beck. Vivid memories of seeing glacial features for the first time, a perspective that a boy in the classroom only imagines, abide from those schoolboy days. The rain was torrential as we worked on the drumlins below Green Tongue. For a treat at the end of one day's work we climbed Stake Pass and the Langdale Pikes (I'm almost ashamed to admit that I do not recall which one), descending via the legendary Dungeon Ghyll. We were even treated to sunshine for our descent from the Pikes and I found my own love affair with the mountains was beginning.

Years later I had the opportunity to revisit Lakeland for a holiday and I filled the week with lowland walks, learning more about the area and wondering what it would be like to visit the peaks and ridges. Soon I was visiting regularly and found that low walks were no longer challenging enough. Harter Fell, Mardale Ill Bell and High Street were my first high level walk as an adult and in succeeding to the summit of Harter Fell I discovered why walkers lose their hearts to the mountains. I too lost mine. I immediately decided to climb all of the Lake District peaks - even though I had no idea how many there were!

So my hobby as a fellwalker began. Days out collecting memories of sublime views and never to be forgotten experiences. I set about equipping myself for my hobby, buying equipment and books as soon as I could afford to.

During the course of my visits to the mountains, I met people of whom memories will forever linger. In 1989, my wife and I met a pensioner as were descending from Scarth Gap to Gatesgarth. He described how, during the previous week, he had just completed ascending all the mountains listed by Wainwright for the second time. He reminisced about past days walking with his wife, who had recently passed away. The mountains reminded him of her since they had constantly walked and climbed together. He left us behind on the descent - we were holding him up!

A second story comes to mind from a windy afternoon on The Nab. As my wife and I sat admiring the northern view along Bannerdale, a stranger came over the top of the fell behind us. We were apprehensive since we had earlier received a verbal rebuff from a worker at the borders of the deer forest, despite possessing permission from the estate owner to allow us to walk on his land. The stranger was clearly nervous as he approached us; it transpired that he was trespassing and had taken us for the landowner! As we chatted over lunch he explained that there were only two Lakeland fells that he had not climbed and that he would be completing those during the next few weeks. I almost felt jealous until I considered the position; I could still look forward, whereas he could not, to the experiences yet to come of further fine first ascents.

What then for him? He would be coming again, revisiting the mountains time after time. Once you have fallen in love with mountain walking the affair does not end because you have visited everything once. You always want to return, exploring different routes and revisiting old favourites.

By now I had started to develop my own rough notebook of walks, recording dates and conditions as I climbed each mountain. Some would need to be re-climbed; perhaps the ascent was in mist or in snow or simply so good that it demanded a second visit and, of course, why use the same ascent for a future visit when alternatives are available?

What I needed was a proper log book to record what I had already done before things went any further. Since there was nothing available in the shops for climbers or walkers so I decided to develop my own. This book is my formula for logging the mountains of England.

I am the first to admit that this book has an arbitrary content. It would have been possible to record more or less information, indeed I cannot claim that I complete my own Log Book rigorously, but I suspect that I will, in future years, look back with disappointment if I do not, so I try hard to keep it up to date. It is my field notebook, my record of happy days on the mountains. Designed not to replace existing guide books, but to complement them and provide a proper place for recording personal achievements. I hope you find it provides a useful record of your walks, which together with your photographs and film, will help to provide a complete memory of your days on the mountains.

Mark Woosey

CONTENTS

Introduction

Explanatory Notes

This book and its companion (*A Log Book of the Mountains of Wales*) are organised into chapters, each being devoted to one of the geographical areas of England or Wales. However, the abundance of mountains in the Lake District means that this entire area has been geographically divided at a lower level. The only exception to this geographical grouping is the Peak District and Dartmoor chapter; here, I simply wished to avoid a chapter consisting of just two mountains, so I amalgamated Dartmoor with the next smallest chapter for purely practical reasons. The order of the mountains within each chapter is alphabetical.

In compiling this book I have presented information on the most commonly used routes. Most of these present few technical problems in good weather conditions. I have assumed that readers are competent navigators and plan their routes according to both the conditions and the abilities of their party.

Descriptions of routes are not provided as that would make the book into a guide rather than a log. This book is intended to supplement existing guides and as such provides the key information about a route: the start point, the distance and the height gained from the start point to the summit.

There is no "official" definition of a mountain and this has clearly perplexed guide book writers in the past. As a consequence different rules have been developed to justify the content of the guide books that have been written. Many authors designate mountains as those over 2000ft. or 600m and usually qualify this with supplementary statements such as "rising above the surroundings by 50ft. or 10m". But this leaves out some of the best walks and in the end remains arbitrary. I have used the 600m lower limit as my start point, but included mountains of a lesser height where I believe they deserve inclusion for their topographical or other merit. So the content is arbitrary here too, but I hope as a result comprehensive, since it includes many of the lower mountains we all love to walk.

Compiling the tables

In the preparation of the tables I have used the most recent Ordnance Survey 1:10 000, 1:25 000 and 1:50,000 maps when pin-pointing the routes and summits. Ordnance Survey place names and spelling have been used throughout and although they themselves are inconsistent, any errors you may find are my own responsibility. I have found that the best maps for walkers are the 1:25 000 Outdoor Leisure, Explorer or Pathfinder series although other publications such as

Bartholomew's provide excellent alternatives for many areas. Details of the required maps are provided for each mountain with a summary at the back of the book.

Distances and Heights

Ascent and ridge distances are, in most instances, rounded up or down to the nearest 0.25km.

Ascent heights are for the vertical gain from the start point to the summit, to the nearest metre. No allowance is normally made for rolling hillsides, the figure provided simply represents the vertical height gain from the start point to the summit. A few routes necessitate two large climbs, such as when ascending Pillar from Gatesgarth via Scarth Gap Pass. Here the first climb is to the top of the pass and the second from Ennerdale to Pillar Summit and when this occurs the height figure is the cumulative amount of height gained. For Ridge Routes a descent from one summit to a low point followed by a climb to the next is invariably the case; these details are provided too.

I have used the modern metric heights as the base figure for mountain heights. However, it is a fact that the height of several mountains appears to have changed both during the metrication of our maps and during recent re-surveying. As a consequence, direct conversion of the imperial figures to metric and vice versa can produce some seemingly incorrect results. Consequently the height of some mountains may appear to be a foot or two higher or lower than they actually are and for that I apologise. I hope I have provided the correct figures.

Access

It has frequently been pointed out that guide book writers ignore rights of way and document routes regardless. I have tried to ensure that all the routes mentioned use public rights of way, permissive paths and those in general use by walkers. However these do alter over time and unfortunately it should be noted that any reference to paths or other lines of ascent does not guarantee that a right of way exists.

Features

I hope I have included all the main features which are of the most interest either intrinsically or for navigating purposes, however space has been left for you to add to the list if necessary.

Completing the tables

Details of all the popular, and some lesser known, routes of ascent and descent are provided. Space exists to record your ascent and descent by any three of these routes for each mountain and to add at least one new route should you so wish - perhaps a scrambling route that I have not included. There are, of course, variations to many of the routes and you should use the Notes space to detail these accordingly.

Any easy method to illustrate how to complete the book is by example, so I have provided two samples below of a singular ascent (**A**) and a circular walk (**B**), the latter taking in two summits and therefore including a ridge route. You can cross reference the text to the sample of the log which follows.

Example One: Haystacks (an ascent and descent of the same mountain)

This example records an ascent of Haystacks from Gatesgarth (on 05.03.95) via Scarth Gap Pass, descending via Warnscale bottom. Details are completed in the first column (**A**) since this is the first ascent of Haystacks.

'Ascent' is noted in 'Scarth Gap Pass' box and **'Descent'** is noted in the 'Warnscale & grass path' box in the Route from section. Features visited are marked with **'Yes'** as appropriate and the completion of Times and Weather is self explanatory.

The Descent took 1hr. 15 mins. so this is noted in the separate Time box.

Example Two: Haystacks and Fleetwith Pike (a ridge walk)

This example records an ascent of Haystacks from Gatesgarth (on 27.03.95) via Warnscale and the Quarry Path and crossing the 'ridge' to Fleetwith Pike from where descent via Fleetwith Edge was made. This is the second ascent of Haystacks so the details are completed in column **B**, but the first ascent for Fleetwith Pike where details are completed in column **A.**

For Haystacks **'Ascent'** is noted in the 'Warnscale and Quarry Path' box in the Route from section. The route then continues to Fleetwith Pike, so **'onto'** is noted in the Ridge Routes section against the Fleetwith Pike heading. Features and Times and Weather are completed as before. The ascent of Haystacks starts at 8.00 am and the summit is reached at 9.20 am. a Duration of 1hr 20 min. There is no descent from Haystacks so the separate Time box is empty.

Switching to the Fleetwith Pike entry reveals a Departure time of 9.30am (this is the departure time from the summit of Haystacks) and an Arrival time of 10.15 am (at Fleetwith Pike summit), a Duration of 45 min. It is also clear from this that 10 mins were spent on the summit of Haystacks. This entry also reveals that the ascent was actually via the Ridge route **'From'** Haystacks. The final **'Descent'** is noted in the 'Gatesgarth/Fleetwith Edge' box and took 40 mins as noted in the Time box.

The principal of recording Departure Time, Arrival time and **From** and **Onto** in the Ridge route section allows you to record your walks along all or part of a summit ridge, noting where you both joined and exited the ridge itself and the individual summits visited.

Haystacks   597m   1959'   NGR NY193132

Route from	A 05:03:95	B 27:03:95		Ascent	Km	Time
Gatesgarth via:						
Scarth Gap Pass	Ascent			477	2.75	
Warnscale & Quarry Road		Ascent		477	4.25	
Warnscale & grass path #	Descent			477	4.0	1hr 15min

Ridge routes				Descent	Ascent	Km
Brandreth				221	103	3.0
Fleetwith Pike		onto		158	107	3.75

Features visited			
Summit cairns (2)	Yes	Yes	
Blackbeck Tarn	Yes	Yes	

Times and Weather			
Departure time	09:00, am.	08.00, am.	
Arrival time	10:30, am.	09:20, am.	
Duration	1hr.30min	1hr.20min	
Weather	Dry, Cold	Dry,Cloud	
Visibility	Good	Clear	

Fleetwith Pike   648m   2126'   NGR NY206142

Route from/via	A 27.03.95			Ascent	Km	Time
Gatesgarth/Fleetwith Edge	Descent			528	1.25	40 mins
Gatesgarth via #				528	4.5	

Ridge routes				Descent	Ascent	Km
Brandreth				180	113	3.5
Grey Knotts				162	113	2.5
Haystacks	From			107	158	3.75

Features visited			
Summit cairn	Yes		
Fanny Mercer's Cross	Yes		

Times and Weather			
Departure time	9:30, am.		
Arrival time	10:15, am		
Duration	45min		
Weather	Dry,Cloud		
Visibility	Average		

Quick Reference

Information Provided

First Table

Route from | The main start points and routes for ascending this mountain (grid references are provided for some locations which otherwise may be difficult to pin-point).

Ascent | The vertical height gain, in metres, between the start point and the summit.

km | The distance, in kilometres, from the start point to the summit following the 'Route from'. It is normally accurate to approximately 0.25km.

Second Table

Ridge Routes | The adjacent mountains from which a ridge walk can be completed. There is not necessarily a well defined path to follow for these routes.

Descent | The height loss, in metres, to the lowest point between two summits on a ridge walk.

Ascent | The height gain, in metres, to the adjacent summit from the lowest point on a ridge walk.

Information to complete

Date of ascent | Recorded at the top of the column, Three ascents are possible in this Log for each mountain.

Main Routes | The route of ascent or descent. Record "Ascent" or (A), or "Descent" or (D) in the box a adjacent to the route used as appropriate.

Ridge Routes | The route of a (normally circular) walk, where you are following a series of summits along a ridge. The conventions used are "onto" and "from". See the example for Haystacks and Fleetwith Pike.

Features visited | Tick those visited or use "Yes" to indicate visited. Additional comments are valid e.g. "inaccessible" as might be the case for Napes Needle.

Departure time | The time you leave the start point for the walk. It can be used to record either:
(1) the time the ascent of the mountain commenced or
(2) the time one summit was departed from en route to another summit - when following a ridge route.

Arrival | The time you arrive at a summit either from a single ascent or another summit when walking a ridge. It is used in association with Departure time. The difference between the two times is Duration.

Duration | The difference between Departure time and Arrival time as mentioned above. Depending on whether departure is from the start of a full ascent or another summit it records either:
(1) the ascent duration or
(2) the summit to summit duration.
    It does not record the descent duration.

Time | The descent time from a summit. If more than one ascent of a mountain is made via the same route you should note which of the dates this descent time applies to. If you wish to record more than one descent time for the same route the Notes section should be used.

Abbreviations

c.p. | Car park
g.r. | Grid reference (779192) Actual grid reference
Y. hostel | Youth hostel   Y.H   Youth hostel

CHAPTER ONE

THE CHEVIOTS and KIELDER

CHEVIOTS

Auchope Cairn   726m   2382'   NGR NT891198
Landranger 80

Route from				Ascent	Km	Time
Cocklawfoot				496	4.5	

Ridge routes				Descent	Ascent	Km
Hangingstone Hill				38	21	.75
The Schil				125	246	4.0

Features visited				Notes _____
Summit cairn				_____
				_____

Times and Weather				_____
Departure time				_____
Arrival time				_____
Duration				_____
Weather				_____
Visibility				_____

Beefstand Hill   561m   1840'   NGR NT821114
Landranger 80

Route from				Ascent	Km	Time
Hownam (779192) #				410	7.0	

Ridge routes				Descent	Ascent	Km
Lamb Hill				16	66	2.0
Mozie Law				27	36	1.0

Features visited				Notes _____
Summit cairn				_____
				_____

Times and Weather				_____
Departure time				_____
Arrival time				_____
Duration				_____
Weather				_____
Visibility				Route Details: # = via Green Hill

Black Hag   549m   1801'   NGR NT862237
Landranger 74

Route from				Ascent	Km	Time
Hethpool				419	8.0	
Kirk Yetholm				447	6.5	
Sourhope				320	4.5	

Ridge routes				Descent	Ascent	Km
The Curr				67	52	1.0
The Schil				125	69	1.25

Features visited				Notes
Summit				

Times and Weather			
Departure time			
Arrival time			
Duration			
Weather			
Visibility			

Bloodybush Edge   610m   2001'   NGR NT902144
Landranger 80

Route from				Ascent	Km	Time
Alwinton				454	10.50	

Ridge routes				Descent	Ascent	Km
Cushat Law				116	110	3.0

Features visited				Notes
O.S. trig. point				

Times and Weather			
Departure time			
Arrival time			
Duration			
Weather			
Visibility			

Cairn Hill   776m   2546'   NGR NT903195
Landranger 80

Route from			Ascent	Km	Time
Langleeford (953225)			576	6.5	
Langleeford Hope (932208)			466	4.0	

Ridge routes			Descent	Ascent	Km
Comb Fell			67	191	1.5
Hangingstone Hill			8	41	.5
The Cheviot			50	11	1.0

Features visited				Notes
Summit cairn				

Times and Weather			
Departure time			
Arrival time			
Duration			
Weather			
Visibility			

The Cheviot   815m   2764'   NGR NT909205
Landranger 74 & 75

Route from			Ascent	Km	Time
Langleeford (953225)			615	6.5	
Langleeford Hope (932208)			505	2.5	
Mounthooly #			520	5.0	

Ridge routes			Descent	Ascent	Km
Cairn Hill			11	50	1.0

Features visited				Notes
Summit cairn				
O.S. trig. point				

Times and Weather			
Departure time			
Arrival time			
Duration			
Weather			
Visibility			

Route details: # = via Hen-Hole direct.

Comb Fell   652m   2139'   NGR NT924187
Landranger 80

Route from				Ascent	Km	Time
High Bleakhope (926158)				372	3.0	

Ridge routes				Descent	Ascent	Km
Cairn Hill				191	67	1.5
Hedgehope Hill				154	90	2.5

Features visited				Notes
Unmarked summit				

Times and Weather			
Departure time			
Arrival time			
Duration			
Weather			
Visibility			

The Curr   564m   1850'   NGR NT851233
Landranger 74

Route from				Ascent	Km	Time
Kirk Yetholm				462	6.5	
Primidemill				429	7.0	
Sourhope				335	3.5	

Ridge routes				Descent	Ascent	Km
Black Hag				52	67	1.0

Features visited				Notes
O.S. trig. point				

Times and Weather			
Departure time			
Arrival time			
Duration			
Weather			
Visibility			

Cushat Law   616m   2021' NGR NT928138
Landranger 80

Route from				Ascent	Km	Time
Alwinton via Forest				460	9	

Ridge routes				Descent	Ascent	Km
Bloodybush Edge				110	116	3.0

Features visited			
Summit cairns			

Times and Weather			
Departure time			
Arrival time			
Duration			
Weather			
Visibility			

Notes _____

Hangingstone Hill   743m   2438' NGR NT896194
Landranger 80

Route from				Ascent	Km	Time

Ridge routes				Descent	Ascent	Km
Auchope Cairn				21	38	.75
Cairn Hill				41	8	.5
Windy Gyle				114	238	6.5

Features visited			
Summit cairn			

Times and Weather			
Departure time			
Arrival time			
Duration			
Weather			
Visibility			

Notes _____

Hedgehope Hill   714m   2348' NGR NT944198
Landranger 74 & 90

Route from				Ascent	Km	Time

Ridge routes				Descent	Ascent	Km
Comb Fell				90	154	2.5

Features visited				Notes _____
Summit cairn				
O.S. trig. point				

Times and Weather			
Departure time			
Arrival time			
Duration			
Weather			
Visibility			

Lamb Hill   511m   1677' NGR NT811137
Landranger 80

Route from				Ascent	Km	Time
Hownam (779192) #				351	7.0	
Pennymuir (755144)				271	7.0	

Ridge routes				Descent	Ascent	Km
Beefstand Hill				66	16	2.0

Features visited				Notes _____
Summit cairn				
O.S. trig. point				

Times and Weather			
Departure time			
Arrival time			
Duration			
Weather			
Visibility			

Route details # = via Green Hill.

Mozie Law   552m   1811' NGR NT829150
Landranger 80

Route from				Ascent	Km	Time
Barrow Burn (868108) #				352	7.0	
Hownam (779192) #				392	9.0	

Ridge routes				Descent	Ascent	Km
Beefstand Hill				36	27	1.0
Windy Gyle				79	12	3.0

Features visited			
Summit cairn			

Times and Weather			
Departure time			
Arrival time			
Duration			
Weather			
Visibility			

Notes _____

Route details: # = via The Street.

The Schil   605m   1985' NGR869223
Landranger 74

Route from				Ascent	Km	Time
Hethpool				465	9.0	
Kirk Yetholm				503	8.0	
Primidemill				470	9.0	
Sourhope (Bowmont Valley)				376	5.5	

Ridge routes				Descent	Ascent	Km
Auchope Cairn				246	125	4.0
Black Hag				69	125	1.25

Features visited			
Summit			

Times and Weather			
Departure time			
Arrival time			
Duration			
Weather			
Visibility			

Notes _____

Windy Gyle   619m   2031'   NGR NT855152
Landranger 80

Route from				Ascent	Km	Time
Alwinton via Clennell St.				463	12.5	
Barrow Burn (867108)				369	6.0	
Cocklawfoot				379	4.0	
Calroust (824192)				399	6.0	
Hownam via The Street				477	9.5	
Mowhaugh				448	7.5	

Ridge routes				Descent	Ascent	Km
Hangingstone Hill				238	114	6.5
Mozie Law				12	79	3.0

Features visited			
Summit (Russell's) cairn			
O.S. trig. point			
Summit windshelter			

Times and Weather			
Departure time			
Arrival time			
Duration			
Weather			
Visibility			

Notes _____

_____

_____

_____

_____

_____

_____

_____

_____

_____

_____

_____

_____

_____

_____

KIELDER

Carlin Tooth   622m   1808'   NGR NT631025
Landranger 80

Route from				Ascent	Km	Time

Ridge routes				Descent	Ascent	Km
Hartshorn Pike				nil	5.0	1.0

Features visited				Notes _____
Summit cairn				
O.S. trig. point				

Times and Weather			
Departure time			
Arrival time			
Duration			
Weather			
Visibility			

Deadwater Fell   569m   1867'   NGR NY626973
Landranger 80   Explorer 1

Route from				Ascent	Km	Time
Deadwater (605969)				349	5.25	
Kielder				369	5.5	

Ridge routes				Descent	Ascent	Km
Mid Fell				46	54	1.25

Features visited				Notes _____
Summit				
O.S. trig. point				

Times and Weather			
Departure time			
Arrival time			
Duration			
Weather			
Visibility			

Hartshorn Pike   545m   1788'   NGR NT626015
Landranger 80

Route from				Ascent	Km	Time

Ridge routes				Descent	Ascent	Km
Carlin Tooth				5	nil	1.0
Peel Fell				107	50	2.0

Features visited				Notes _____
Summit cairn				

Times and Weather			
Departure time			
Arrival time			
Duration			
Weather			
Visibility			

Mid Fell   561m   1841'   NGR NT636984
Landranger 80   Explorer 1

Route from				Ascent	Km	Time

Ridge routes				Descent	Ascent	Km
Deadwater Fell				54	46	1.25
Peel Fell				67	23	2.0

Features visited				Notes _____
Summit cairn/shelter				

Times and Weather			
Departure time			
Arrival time			
Duration			
Weather			
Visibility			

Peel Fell   602m   1975'   NGR NY626998
Landranger 80   Explorer 1

Route from				Ascent	Km	Time
Deadwater (605969) #				382	5.0	

Ridge routes				Descent	Ascent	Km
Hartshorn Pike				50	107	2.0
Mid Fell				23	67	2.0

Features visited			
Summit cairn			

Times and Weather			
Departure time			
Arrival time			
Duration			
Weather			
Visibility			

Notes _____

_____

_____

_____

_____

_____

_____

_____

_____

_____

_____

Route details: # = via forest track.

CHAPTER TWO

PENNINES

Mountain	Page	Height in Metres	Date first Ascended
Backstone Edge	19	699	___:___:___
Bellbeaver Rigg	19	620	___:___:___
Bink Moss	20	619	___:___:___
Black Fell	21	664	___:___:___
Black Hill	21	645	___:___:___
Bullman Hills	22	610	___:___:___
Burnhope Seat	22	746	___:___:___
Burtree Fell	23	612	___:___:___
Chapfell Top	23	703	___:___:___
Cold Fell	24	621	___:___:___
Croglin Fell	24	591	___:___:___
Cross Fell	25	893	___:___:___
Dead Stones	26	710	___:___:___
The Dodd	26	614	___:___:___
Fendrith Hill	27	696	___:___:___
Fiend's Fell	27	634	___:___:___
Flinty Fell	28	614	___:___:___
Great Dun Fell	28	848	___:___:___
Great Stony Hill	29	708	___:___:___
Grey Nag	29	656	___:___:___
Harwood Common	30	718	___:___:___
Killhope Law	30	673	___:___:___
Knock Fell	31	794	___:___:___
Knoutberry Hill	31	668	___:___:___
Little Dun Fell	32	842	___:___:___
Little Fell	32	748	___:___:___
Long Man Hill	33	658	___:___:___
Meldon Hill	33	767	___:___:___
Melmerby Fell	34	709	___:___:___
Mickle Fell	34	788	___:___:___
Middlehope Moor	35	612	___:___:___
Murton Fell	35	675	___:___:___
Outberry Plain	36	653	___:___:___
Round Hill	36	686	___:___:___
Scaud Hill	37	694	___:___:___
Thack Moor	37	609	___:___:___
Three Pikes	38	651	___:___:___
Tom Smith's Stone	38	637	___:___:___
Viewing Hill	39	649	___:___:___
Watch Hill	39	602	___:___:___
Westernhope Moor	40	675	___:___:___

Backstone Edge   699m   2293'   NGR NY726277
Landranger 91   Outdoor Leisure 31

Route from				Ascent	Km	Time
Dufton				524	5.25+	

Ridge routes				Descent	Ascent	Km
Knock Fell				129	34	2.75
Meldon Hill				142	74	4.75

Features visited			
Summit cairn			
O.S. trig. point			

Times and Weather			
Departure time			
Arrival time			
Duration			
Weather			
Visibility			

Notes _____
_____
_____
_____
_____
_____
_____
_____
_____

Bellbeaver Rigg   620m   2034'   NGR NY763351
(Tynehead Fell) Landranger 91   Outdoor Leisure 31

Route from				Ascent	Km	Time
Cow Green Res'r. (811309)				110	8.0	
Dorthgillfoot (757384)				170	4.0	
Hill House Farm (757386)				170	4.5	
B6277 @ 781358				30	2.5	

Ridge routes				Descent	Ascent	Km
Burnhope Seat				156	30	5.0
Knock Fell				264	90	8.0
Round Hill				129	63	2.5
Viewing Hill				75	95	3.0

Features visited			
Summit cairns (2)			

Times and Weather			
Departure time			
Arrival time			
Duration			
Weather			
Visibility			

Notes _____
_____
_____
_____
_____
_____
_____
_____
_____

Bink Moss   619m   2031'   NGR NY875243
Landranger 91   Outdoor Leisure 31

Route from/via				Ascent	Km	Time
High Force/Hagworm Hill				319	6.5	
High Force/Green Fell				319	7.5	
B6267 @ Hargill Bridge #				238	3.25	
B6267 Footpath nr. above *				244	4.5	

Ridge routes/via				Descent	Ascent	Km
Mickle Fell/Danger Area				208	39	7.5

Features visited			
Summit			
O.S. marker (obsolete)			
Hagworm Hill (597m)			
Green Fell			
Cauldron Snout			
High Force			
Low Force			

Times and Weather			
Departure time			
Arrival time			
Duration			
Weather			
Visibility			

Notes _____

_____

_____

_____

_____

_____

_____

_____

_____

_____

Route details: # = bridge is located @ G.R. 885217, * = Footpath West of Hargill Bridge, starts @ G.R. 882214.

Black Fell   664m   2179'   NGR NY648444
Landranger 86

Route from				Ascent	Km	Time
Hartside Cross				84	2.75	
Howgill Rigg (702483)				402	7.5	
Renwick (596435)				464	6.0	

Ridge routes				Descent	Ascent	Km
Fiend's Fell				54	84	4.0
Tom Smith's Stone				22	49	3.0
Watch Hill				47	109	4.75

Features visited			
O.S. trig. point			

Notes _____

Times and Weather			
Departure time			
Arrival time			
Duration			
Weather			
Visibility			

Black Hill   645m   2116'   NGR NY906334
Landranger 91   Outdoor Leisure 31

Route from				Ascent	Km	Time
Swinhope Head (897332)				38	.75	

Ridge routes				Descent	Ascent	Km
Fendrith Hill				89	38	3.0
Westernhope Moor				40	10	2.0

Features visited			
Summit cairn			
O.S. trig. point			

Notes _____

Times and Weather			
Departure time			
Arrival time			
Duration			
Weather			
Visibility			

Bullman Hills   610m   2001'   NGR NY705371
Landranger 91   Outdoor Leisure 31

Route from				Ascent	Km	Time
Garrigill				267	8.0C	

Ridge routes				Descent	Ascent	Km
Cross Fell				293	10	4.0
Little Dun Fell				237	5	7.5
Long Man Hill				48	nil	2.5

Features visited				Notes _____
Summit cairn				

Times and Weather			
Departure time			
Arrival time			
Duration			
Weather			
Visibility			

Burnhope Seat   746m   2448'   NGR NY788375
Landranger 91   Outdoor Leisure 31

Route from				Ascent	Km	Time
Cow Green Res'r (811309)				246	9.0	
Darngill Bridge (774371)				166	1.5	
B6277 @ 781357				156	2.5	

Ridge routes				Descent	Ascent	Km
Bellbeaver Rigg				30	155	5.0
Dead Stones				33	69	2.5
Harwood Common				13	41	1.5

Features visited				Notes _____
Summit cairn (West of trig. pt.)				
O.S. trig. point				

Times and Weather			
Departure time			
Arrival time			
Duration			
Weather			
Visibility			

Burtree Fell   612m   2008' NGR NY862432

Landranger 87 Outdoor Leisure 31

Route from				Ascent	Km	Time
Allenheads				202	3.5	
Burtree Ford				234	2.75	

Features visited			
Summit cairn			

Notes _____

Times and Weather			
Departure time			
Arrival time			
Duration			
Weather			
Visibility			

Chapfell Top   703m   2306' NGR NY876346

(Langdon Fell) Landranger 91 Outdoor Leisure 31

Route from				Ascent	Km	Time
Harthope Head (862350)				73	1.5	
Swinhope Bridge (895346)				260	1.25	

Ridge routes				Descent	Ascent	Km
Fendrith Hill				11	17	1.25

Features visited			
Summit cairn			

Notes _____

Times and Weather			
Departure time			
Arrival time			
Duration			
Weather			
Visibility			

Cold Fell   621m   2037'   NGR NY606556
Landranger 86

Route from				Ascent	Km	Time
Hallbankgate				421	5.0	
Midgeholme (A689)				418	5.0	
Tindale Tarn				405	4.5	

Features visited			
Summit cairn			
O.S. trig. point			

Times and Weather			
Departure time			
Arrival time			
Duration			
Weather			
Visibility			

Notes _____
_____
_____
_____
_____
_____
_____
_____
_____
_____

Croglin Fell   591m   1939'   NGR NY596495
(summit called Blotting Raise) Landranger 86

Route from				Ascent	Km	Time
Croglin				391	4.25	

Ridge routes				Descent	Ascent	Km
Tom Smith's Stone				112	66	7.0

Features visited			
O.S. trig. point			
Secondary summit (566m) #			

Times and Weather			
Departure time			
Arrival time			
Duration			
Weather			
Visibility			

Notes _____
_____
_____
_____
_____
_____
_____

Route details: # = located at
G.R. 615489.

Cross Fell   893m   2930'   NGR NY687343
Landranger 91   Outdoor Leisure 31

Route from/via				Ascent	Km	Time
Blencarn				723	8.25	
Garrighill (746412)				550	11.5	
Kirkland				690	6.5	
Knock (676274)				815	11.0	
Milburn				703	8.0	
Skirwith via Burrell Hill				747	8.5	
Skirwith via Kirkland				747	9.75	
Townhead via Megs Cairn #				680	9.0	
A686 (676423)/Maiden Way				417	10.0+	

Ridge routes				Descent	Ascent	Km
Bullman Hills				10	293	5.0
Little Dun Fell				70	121	2.25
Long Man Hill				48	283	5.0
Melmerby Fell				41	225	5.25
Round Hill				71	278	6.5

Features visited			
Summit cairn			
O.S. trig. point			
Summit shelter			

Times and Weather			
Departure time			
Arrival time			
Duration			
Weather			
Visibility			

Notes _____
_____
_____
_____
_____
_____
_____
_____
_____
_____
_____
_____

Route details: # = route starts @ G. R. 635340.

Dead Stones   710m   2330'   NGR NY794399
Landranger 91   Outdoor Leisure 31

Route from				Ascent	Km	Time
Blackcleugh (850396)				320	6.0	
Burnhope Reservoir				320	5.5	

Ridge routes/via				Descent	Ascent	Km
Burnhope Seat				69	33	2.5
Flinty Fell/Hunters Cleugh				59	155	4.25
Knoutberry Hill				13	55	2.5

Features visited				Notes _____
Summit cairn				_____
Summit hut				_____
Highwatch Currick (639m)				_____
				_____

Times and Weather				_____
Departure time				_____
Arrival time				_____
Duration				_____
Weather				_____
Visibility				_____

The Dodd   614m   2016'   NGR NY791458
Landranger 87   Outdoor Leisure 31

Route from				Ascent	Km	Time
Carr Shield (806474)				214	2.5	
Coalcleugh				84	1.75	
Nenthead				176	3.25	
Nentsberry (765455)				324	3.0	

Ridge routes				Descent	Ascent	Km
Killhope Law #				88	29	4.5
Killhope Law *				142	83	3.5

Features visited				Notes _____
Summit cairn				_____
				_____

Times and Weather				_____
Departure time				_____
Arrival time				_____
Duration				_____
Weather				Route details: # = via Black Hill
Visibility				Quarries, * = via Coalcleugh.

Fendrith Hill   696m   2284'   NGR NY877333
Landranger 91   Outdoor Leisure 31

Route from				Ascent	Km	Time
Swinhope Head (897332)				89	2.0	

Ridge routes				Descent	Ascent	Km
Black Hill				38	89	3.0
Chapfell Top				17	11	1.25
Westernhope Moor #				68	89	5.0

Features visited			
O.S. trig. point			

Times and Weather			
Departure time			
Arrival time			
Duration			
Weather			
Visibility			

Notes _____
_____
_____
_____
_____
_____
_____

Route details: # = really a ridge
route via Black Hill.

Fiend's Fell   634m   2080'   NGR NY643406
(Gamblesby Allotments) Landranger 86

Route from				Ascent	Km	Time
Hartside Cross				54	1.25	
A686 (628411)				214	2.0	

Ridge routes/via				Descent	Ascent	Km
Black Fell/Hartside Cross				84	54	4.0
Melmerby Fell				104	29	2.5

Features visited			
O.S. trig. point			

Times and Weather			
Departure time			
Arrival time			
Duration			
Weather			
Visibility			

Notes _____
_____
_____
_____
_____
_____
_____
_____

Flinty Fell   614m   2015' NGR NY771420
Landranger 86 & 87   Outdoor Leisure 31

Route from				Ascent	Km	Time
Ashgill Bridge (779405)				194	3.0	
Nenthead				176	3.5	
Minor road @ 766424				46	.75	

Ridge routes				Descent	Ascent	Km
Dead Stones #				155	59	4.25
Knoutberry Hill *				93	39	3.5

Features visited				Notes
Summit				

Times and Weather			
Departure time			
Arrival time			
Duration			
Weather			
Visibility			

Route details: # = via Hunters
Cleugh, * = via Perry's Dam.

Great Dun Fell   848m   2782' NGR NY710322
Landranger 91   Outdoor Leisure 31

Route from				Ascent	Km	Time
Dorthgill Foot (758384)				398	12.0	
Knock				643	7.75	
Milburn				653	5.5	

Ridge routes				Descent	Ascent	Km
Little Dun Fell				62	68	1.25
Knock Fell				49	103	2.5

Features visited				Notes
Summit				
Radar Station				

Times and Weather			
Departure time			
Arrival time			
Duration			
Weather			
Visibility			

Great Stony Hill   708m   2323'   NGR NY824359
Landranger 91   Outdoor Leisure 31

Route from				Ascent	Km	Time
Hawk Sike Hush (814349)				153	2.0	

Ridge routes				Descent	Ascent	Km
Harwood Common #				63	53	3.0
Scaud Hill				39	53	2.25
Three Pikes				30	87	2.75

Features visited			
Summit cairn			
O.S. trig. point			

Notes _____
_____
_____
_____

Times and Weather			
Departure time			
Arrival time			.
Duration			
Weather			
Visibility			

_____
_____
_____
_____
_____

Route details: # = via Scaud Hill
(not a true ridge route).

Grey Nag   656m   2152'   NGR NY665476
Landranger 86

Route from				Ascent	Km	Time
Castle Nook (696490)				361	3.25	
Howgill Rigg (702483)				394	5.0	

Ridge routes				Descent	Ascent	Km
Tom Smith's Stone				31	12	1.25

Features visited			
Summit cairn			
O.S. trig. point			

Notes _____
_____
_____
_____

Times and Weather			
Departure time			
Arrival time			
Duration			
Weather			
Visibility			

_____
_____
_____
_____
_____

Harwood Common   718m   2356' NGR NY795363
Landranger 91   Outdoor Leisure 31

Route from				Ascent	Km	Time
Crookburn Bridge (781358)				128	2.0	

Ridge routes				Descent	Ascent	Km
Burnhope Seat				41	13	1.5
Great Stony Hill #				53	63	3.0
Scaud Hill				9	24	1.25

Features visited			
Summit cairn			

Times and Weather			
Departure time			
Arrival time			
Duration			
Weather			
Visibility			

Notes _____
_____
_____
_____
_____
_____
_____

Route details: # = via Scaud Hill
(not a true ridge route).

Killhope Law   673m   2208' NGR NY819448
Landranger 87   Outdoor Leisure 31

Route from				Ascent	Km	Time
Allenheads				273	5.0	
Killhope				203	2.5	

Ridge routes				Descent	Ascent	Km
The Dodd #				29	88	4.5
The Dodd *				83	142	3.5
Knoutberry Hill				45	50	4.5
Middlehope Moor				42	108	6.0

Features visited			
Summit cairn & pole			
O.S. trig. point			

Times and Weather			
Departure time			
Arrival time			
Duration			
Weather			
Visibility			

Notes _____
_____
_____
_____
_____
_____
_____
_____

Route details: # = via Black Hill
Quarries, * = via Coalcleugh.

Knock Fell 794m 2605' NGR NY722303
Landranger 91   Outdoor Leisure 31

Route from				Ascent	Km	Time
Dufton				619	6.5	
Knock				588	5.5	

Ridge routes				Descent	Ascent	Km
Backstone Edge				34	129	2.75
Bellbeaver Rigg				90	264	8.0
Great Dun Fell				103	49	2.5
Meldon Hill				62	89	5.5
Round Hill				145	254	10.0

Features visited			
Summit cairn			
Knock Old Man (cairn)			

Times and Weather			
Departure time			
Arrival time			
Duration			
Weather			
Visibility			

Notes _____
_____
_____
_____
_____
_____
_____
_____
_____

Knoutberry Hill 668m 2192' NGR NY802421
Landranger 87   Outdoor Leisure 31

Route from				Ascent	Km	Time
Killhope Cross (799432)				45	1.5	

Ridge routes				Descent	Ascent	Km
Dead Stones				55	13	2.5
Flinty Fell #				39	93	3.5
Killhope Law				50	45	4.5

Features visited			
Summit			

Times and Weather			
Departure time			
Arrival time			
Duration			
Weather			
Visibility			

Notes _____
_____
_____
_____
_____
_____
_____
_____

Route details: # = via Perry's Dam.

Little Dun Fell   842m   2763'   NGR NY704330
Landranger 91   Outdoor Leisure 31

Route from				Ascent	Km	Time
Blencarn				672	8.0	
Milburn				647	6.0	

Ridge routes				Descent	Ascent	Km
Bullman Hills				5	237	7.5
Cross Fell				121	70	2.25
Great Dun Fell				68	62	1.25
Long Man Hill				48	232	6.25
Round Hill				71	227	6.5

Features visited				Notes _____
Summit cairn				

Times and Weather			
Departure time			
Arrival time			
Duration			
Weather			
Visibility			

Little Fell   748m   2454' NGR NY781223
(Hilton Fell/Burton Fell/Warcop Fell) Landranger 91   Outdoor Leisure 31

Route from				Ascent	Km	Time
Cow Green Res'r. (811309)				238	12.5c	
Hilton (734206)				514	6.25	
Murton (728217)				505	6.5	

Ridge routes				Descent	Ascent	Km
Mickle Fell				83	123	3.0
Murton Fell				75	148	3.75c

Features visited				Notes _____
O.S. trig. point				

Times and Weather			
Departure time			
Arrival time			
Duration			
Weather			
Visibility			

Long Man Hill   658m   2159'   NGR NY723373
Landranger 91   Outdoor Leisure 31

Route from				Ascent	Km	Time
Garrigill				315	5.5	

Ridge routes				Descent	Ascent	Km
Bullman Hills				nil	48	2.5
Cross Fell				283	48	5.0
Little Dun Fell				232	48	6.25
Round Hill				136	108	2.5

Features visited			
Summit			

Times and Weather			
Departure time			
Arrival time			
Duration			
Weather			
Visibility			

Notes _____
_____
_____
_____
_____
_____
_____
_____
_____
_____

Meldon Hill   767m   2517'   NGR NY772291
Landranger 91   Outdoor Leisure 31

Route from				Ascent	Km	Time
Dufton via High Cup Nick				580	9.5	
Cow Green Res'r. (810309)				280	6.8	

Ridge routes				Descent	Ascent	Km
Backstone Edge				74	142	4.75
Knock Fell				89	62	5.5

Features visited			
Summit cairn			
O.S. trig. point			

Times and Weather			
Departure time			
Arrival time			
Duration			
Weather			
Visibility			

Notes _____
_____
_____
_____
_____
_____
_____
_____
_____
_____

Melmerby Fell   709m   2326'   NGR NY652380
Landranger 91

Route from				Ascent	Km	Time
Gamblesby				519	5.0	
Melmerby				539	5.0	
Row (628346)				519	5.25	
Townhead (635340)				494	5.0	
A686 (676423)				233	5.5	

Ridge routes				Descent	Ascent	Km
Cross Fell				225	41	5.25
Fiend's Fell				29	104	2.5

Features visited				Notes _____
Summit cairn				_____
Small stone shelter				_____
				_____
				_____

Times and Weather				
Departure time				_____
Arrival time				_____
Duration				_____
Weather				_____
Visibility				_____

Mickle Fell   788m   2585'   NGR NY804243
Landranger 91   Outdoor Leisure 31

Route from				Ascent	Km	Time
Cow Green Res'r. (811309)				278	9.0	

Ridge routes				Descent	Ascent	Km
Bink Moss				39	208	7.5
Little Fell				123	83	3.0
Murton Fell				165	283	7.0

Features visited				Notes _____
Summit cairn				_____
O.S. trig. point (near summit)				_____
				_____

Times and Weather				
Departure time				_____
Arrival time				_____
Duration				_____
Weather				_____
Visibility				_____

Middlehope Moor   612m   2008'   NGR NY862432
Landranger 87   Outdoor Leisure 31

Route from/via				Ascent	Km	Time
Cowshill				250	4.0	
Allenheads/Weardale Way				212	4.0	

Ridge routes				Descent	Ascent	Km
Killhope Law				108	42	6.0

Features visited			
Summit stones			
O.S. trig. point			

Times and Weather			
Departure time			
Arrival time			
Duration			
Weather			
Visibility			

Notes _____

Murton Fell   675m   2215'   NGR NY754246
Landranger 91   Outdoor Leisure 31

Route from				Ascent	Km	Time
Dufton via High Cup Nick				490	8.0	
Hilton (734206)				441	6.5	
Murton (728217)				432	4.25	

Ridge routes				Descent	Ascent	Km
Little Fell				148	75	3.75c
Mickle Fell				283	165	7.0c

Features visited			
Summit cairn			

Times and Weather			
Departure time			
Arrival time			
Duration			
Weather			
Visibility			

Notes _____

Outberry Plain   653m   2142'   NGR NY939331
Landranger 91 & 92   Outdoor Leisure 31

Route from				Ascent	Km	Time

Ridge routes				Descent	Ascent	Km
Westernhope Moor				22	nil	1.5

Features visited				Notes _____
Summit				_____
				_____

Times and Weather				_____
Departure time				_____
Arrival time				_____
Duration				_____
Weather				_____
Visibility				_____

Round Hill   686m   2251'   NGR NY744361
Landranger 86   Outdoor Leisure 31

Route from				Ascent	Km	Time
Dorthgillfoot (757384)				236	3.5	
Garrighill via Pennine Way				343	10.0	
Garrighill via Dorthgillfoot				236	7.0	

Ridge routes				Descent	Ascent	Km
Bellbeaver Rigg				63	129	2.5
Cross Fell				278	71	6.5
Knock Fell				254	145	10.0
Little Dun Fell				227	71	6.5
Long Man Hill				108	136	2.5

Features visited				Notes _____
Summit (Boundary Stone)				_____
Noonstones Hill summit				_____
				_____

Times and Weather				_____
Departure time				_____
Arrival time				_____
Duration				_____
Weather				_____
Visibility				_____

Scaud Hill   694m   2277'   NGR NY804368
Landranger 91   Outdoor Leisure 31

Route from				Ascent	Km	Time
Hawk Sike Hush (814349)				139	2.5	

Ridge routes				Descent	Ascent	Km
Great Stony Hill				53	39	2.25
Harwood Common				24	9	1.25

Features visited			
Summit cairn			

Times and Weather			
Departure time			
Arrival time			
Duration			
Weather			
Visibility			

Notes _____

Thack Moor   609m   1998'   NGR NY612463
(Renwick Fell) Landranger 86

Route from				Ascent	Km	Time
Croglin				409	5.0	
Renwick (596435)				409	3.25	

Ridge routes				Descent	Ascent	Km
Watch Hill				27	34	1.5

Features visited			
Summit cairn			
O.S. trig. point			

Times and Weather			
Departure time			
Arrival time			
Duration			
Weather			
Visibility			

Notes _____

Three Pikes   651m   2136'   NGR NY834343
Landranger 91   Outdoor Leisure 31

Route from				Ascent	Km	Time
Rough Rigg B6277 (821342)				135	1.25	
Ireshope Burn #				322	7.0	

Ridge routes				Descent	Ascent	Km
Great Stony Hill				87	30	2.75

Features visited			
Summit			

Times and Weather			
Departure time			
Arrival time			
Duration			
Weather			
Visibility			

Notes _____

Route details: # = via Grasshill Causeway.

Tom Smith's Stone   637m   2090'   NGR NY655467
Landranger 86

Route from				Ascent	Km	Time
Howgill Rigg (702483)				375	6.5	

Ridge routes				Descent	Ascent	Km
Black Fell				49	22	3.0
Croglin Fell				66	112	7.0
Grey Nag				12	31	1.25
Watch Hill				2	37	3.5

Features visited			
Unmarked summit			
Tom Smith's Stone			

Times and Weather			
Departure time			
Arrival time			
Duration			
Weather			
Visibility			

Notes _____

Viewing Hill   649m   2129'   NGR NY788332
(Herdship Fell)   Landranger 91   Outdoor Leisure 31

Route from				Ascent	Km	Time
Cow Green Res'r. (811309)				139	3.5	
B6277 @ 781358				59	2.75	

Ridge routes				Descent	Ascent	Km
Bellbeaver Rigg				95	75	3.0

Features visited			
Summit cairn			

Times and Weather			
Departure time			
Arrival time			
Duration			
Weather			
Visibility			

Notes _____

Watch Hill   602m   1975'   NGR NY628460
Landranger 86

Route from				Ascent	Km	Time
Renwick (596435)				402	5.0	

Ridge routes				Descent	Ascent	Km
Black Fell				109	47	4.75
Thack Moor				34	27	1.5
Tom Smith's Stone				37	2	3.5

Features visited			
Summit			
Lowthian Jnr. Memorial			

Times and Weather			
Departure time			
Arrival time			
Duration			
Weather			
Visibility			

Notes _____

Westernhope Moor   675m   2215'   NGR NY923326
Landranger 91

Route from				Ascent	Km	Time
Newbiggin				445	6.0	
Swinhope Head (897332)				68	3.0	

Ridge routes				Descent	Ascent	Km
Black Hill				10	40	2.0
Fendrith Hill #				89	68	5.0
Outberry Plain				nil	22	1.5

Features visited			
Summit cairn			
O.S. trig. point			

Times and Weather			
Departure time			
Arrival time			
Duration			
Weather			
Visibility			

Notes _____

_____

_____

_____

_____

_____

_____

_____

Route details: # = really a ridge
route via Black Hill.

CHAPTER THREE

YORKSHIRE DALES

Mountain	Page	Height in Metres	Date first Ascended
Arant Haw	42	606	___:___:___
Archy Styrigg	42	695	___:___:___
Baugh Fell	43	678	___:___:___
Birks Fell	43	610	___:___:___
Bram Rigg Top (Howgills)	44	672	___:___:___
Buckden Pike	44	702	___:___:___
Bush Howe (Howgills)	45	623	___:___:___
Calders (Howgills)	45	674	___:___:___
The Calf (Howgills)	46	676	___:___:___
Crag Hill	46	682	___:___:___
Darnbrook Fell	47	624	___:___:___
Dodd Fell Hill	47	668	___:___:___
Drumaldrace	48	614	___:___:___
Fell Head (Howgills)	48	640	___:___:___
Fountains Fell	49	668	___:___:___
Gragareth	49	627	___:___:___
Great Coum	50	687	___:___:___
Great Knoutberry Hill	50	672	___:___:___
Great Shunner Fell	51	716	___:___:___
Great Whernside	52	704	___:___:___
Green Hill	52	628	___:___:___
High Pike Hill	53	642	___:___:___
High Seat	53	709	___:___:___
Hugh Seat	54	688	___:___:___
Ingleborough	55	723	___:___:___
Knoutberry Haw	56	676	___:___:___
Little Fell	56	667	___:___:___
Lovely Seat	57	675	___:___:___
Nine Standards Rigg	57	662	___:___:___
Pen-y-ghent	58	694	___:___:___
Plover Hill	58	680	___:___:___
Randygill Top (Howgills)	59	624	___:___:___
Rise Hill	59	556	___:___:___
Rogan's Seat	60	672	___:___:___
Sails	60	666	___:___:___
Simon Fell	61	650	___:___:___
Swarth Fell	61	681	___:___:___
Tor Mere Top	62	617	___:___:___
Water Crag	62	668	___:___:___
Whernside	63	736	___:___:___
Wild Boar Fell	64	708	___:___:___
Yarlside (Howgills)	64	639	___:___:___
Yockenthwaite Moor	65	643	___:___:___

Arant Haw   606m 1988' NGR SD662946
Landranger 98

Route from				Ascent	Km	Time
Sedbergh				493	3.5	

Ridge routes				Descent	Ascent	Km
Calders				119	51	2.0

Features visited				Notes _____
Summit cairn				_____
				_____

Times and Weather				_____
Departure time				_____
Arrival time				_____
Duration				_____
Weather				_____
Visibility				_____

Archy Styrigg   695m 2280' NGR NY802004
Landranger 91 & 98

Route from				Ascent	Km	Time
Outhgill				445	3.0	

Ridge routes				Descent	Ascent	Km
High Seat				44	20	1.0
Hugh Seat				18	25	2.0

Features visited				Notes _____
Summit cairn				_____
Gregory Chapel (cairn)				_____
				_____

Times and Weather				_____
Departure time				_____
Arrival time				_____
Duration				_____
Weather				_____
Visibility				_____

Baugh Fell   678m   2224'   NGR SD741916
(Tarn Rig Hill) Landranger 98   Outdoor Leisure 2

Route from				Ascent	Km	Time
A684 @ 694913 #				536	6.0	

Ridge routes				Descent	Ascent	Km
Knoutberry Haw				23	21	1.0
Swarth Fell				381	378	6.0

Features visited			
Summit			
Uldale Force			

Times and Weather			
Departure time			
Arrival time			
Duration			
Weather			
Visibility			

Notes _____
_____
_____
_____
_____
_____
_____
_____
_____

Route details # = via Knoutberry Haw.

Birks Fell   610m   2001'   NGR SD916764
Landranger 98

Route from				Ascent	Km	Time
Hubberholme				370	2.0	
Litton				510	3.75	
Redmire (935774)				440	4.0	

Features visited			
Summit			
Birks Tarn			

Times and Weather			
Departure time			
Arrival time			
Duration			
Weather			
Visibility			

Notes _____
_____
_____
_____
_____
_____
_____
_____
_____

Bram Rigg Top   672m   2205'   NGR SD668965
Landranger 98

Route from				Ascent	Km	Time
Birkhaw (638947)				492	4.0	

Ridge routes				Descent	Ascent	Km
Calders				19	17	.75
The Calf				36	32	.5

Features visited			
Summit cairn			

Times and Weather			
Departure time			
Arrival time			
Duration			
Weather			
Visibility			

Notes _____
_____
_____
_____
_____
_____
_____
_____
_____
_____
_____
_____

Buckden Pike   702m   2303'   NGR SD961788
Landranger 98   Outdoor Leisure 30

Route from				Ascent	Km	Time
Buckden				470	3.0	
Kettlewell				492	8.0	
Starbottom #				472	4.5	
Starbottom *				472	6.0	

Ridge routes				Descent	Ascent	Km
Great Whernside				214	212	7.5
Tor Mere Top				12	87	2.75

Features visited			
Summit cairn			
O.S. trig. point			
Memorial Cross (962778)			

Times and Weather			
Departure time			
Arrival time			
Duration			
Weather			
Visibility			

Notes _____
_____
_____
_____
_____
_____
_____
_____

Route details: # = via Walden
Road, * = via Starbottom Cam
Road.

Bush Howe   623m   2044'   NGR SD659981
Landranger 97

Route from				Ascent	Km	Time
Howgill				428	4.25	

Ridge routes				Descent	Ascent	Km
The Calf				71	18	1.75
Fell Head				85	68	3.0
Randygill Top				254	253	5.0

Features visited			
Summit cairn			

Times and Weather			
Departure time			
Arrival time			
Duration			
Weather			
Visibility			

Notes _____
_____
_____
_____
_____
_____
_____
_____
_____
_____
_____

Calders   674m   2211'   NGR SD671961
Landranger 98

Route from				Ascent	Km	Time
Low Haygarth (697966)				484	2.5	
Sedbergh				561	5.25	

Ridge routes				Descent	Ascent	Km
Arant Haw				51	119	2.0
Bram Rigg Top				17	19	.75

Features visited			
Summit cairn			

Times and Weather			
Departure time			
Arrival time			
Duration			
Weather			
Visibility			

Notes _____
_____
_____
_____
_____
_____
_____
_____
_____
_____

The Calf   676m   2218'   NGR SD667971
Landranger 98

Route from				Ascent	Km	Time
Birkhaw (638947)				496	4.0	
Howgill (632959)				481	4.0	
Low Haygarth (697967)				486	3.5	
Sedbergh				546	6.25	

Ridge routes				Descent	Ascent	Km
Bram Rigg Top				32	36	.5
Bush Howe				18	71	1.75
Yarlside				219	256	3.0

Features visited			
O.S. trig. point			
Cautley Spout			

Times and Weather			
Departure time			
Arrival time			
Duration			
Weather			
Visibility			

Notes _____

Crag Hill   682m   2238'   NGR SD692833
Landranger 98   Outdoor Leisure 2

Route from				Ascent	Km	Time
Dent				532	4.5	

Ridge routes				Descent	Ascent	Km
Great Coum				12	7	1.0

Features visited			
O.S. trig. point			

Times and Weather			
Departure time			
Arrival time			
Duration			
Weather			
Visibility			

Notes _____

Darnbrook Fell   624m   2047'   NGR SD885278
Landranger 98   Outdoor Leisure 2 & 30

Route from				Ascent	Km	Time
Foxup				316	9.5	
Halton Gill				326	9.0	
Litton				374	3.0	
Malham Tarn Field Centre				234	8.0	

Ridge routes				Descent	Ascent	Km
Fountains Fell				84	40	2.75

Features visited			
O.S. trig. point			

Times and Weather			
Departure time			
Arrival time			
Duration			
Weather			
Visibility			

Notes _____
_____
_____
_____
_____
_____
_____
_____
_____
_____

Dodd Fell Hill   668m   2192'   NGR SD841846
Landranger 98   Outdoor Leisure 2 & 30

Route from				Ascent	Km	Time
Gayle #				408	7.5	
Gayle *				408	6.5	

Ridge routes				Descent	Ascent	Km
Drumaldrace				73	127	5.0

Features visited			
O.S. trig. point			
Aysgill Force			

Times and Weather			
Departure time			
Arrival time			
Duration			
Weather			
Visibility			

Notes _____
_____
_____
_____
_____
_____

Route details: # = via
Beggarmans Road, * = via West
Cam Road (Pennine Way).

Drumaldrace   614m   2014'   NGR SD874867
(Wether Fell) Landranger 98   Outdoor Leisure 2 & 30

Route from/via				Ascent	Km	Time
Bainbridge/Cam High Road				395	7.5	
Burtersett				320	3.5	
Countersett				319	5.25	
Gayle				354	4.0	
Marsett (903863)				349	3.5	

Ridge routes				Descent	Ascent	Km
Dodd Fell Hill				127	73	5.0

Features visited			
Summit cairn			

Notes _____
_____
_____
_____

Times and Weather			
Departure time			
Arrival time			
Duration			
Weather			
Visibility			

_____
_____
_____
_____
_____
_____

Fell Head   640m   2100'   NGR SD650982
Landranger 97

Route from				Ascent	Km	Time
Beck House (634967)				440	2.75	

Ridge routes				Descent	Ascent	Km
Bush Howe				68	85	3.0

Features visited			
Summit cairn			

Notes _____
_____
_____
_____

Times and Weather			
Departure time			
Arrival time			
Duration			
Weather			
Visibility			

_____
_____
_____
_____
_____
_____

Fountains Fell   668m   2192'   NGR SD864716
Landranger 98   Outdoor Leisure 2

Route from				Ascent	Km	Time
Foxup				360	8.0	
Halton Gill				370	8.0	
Malham Tarn Field Centre				278	7.0	
Stainforth #				466	8.5	

Ridge routes				Descent	Ascent	Km
Darnbrook Fell				40	84	2.75
Pen-y-ghent				270	238	6.0

Features visited			
Summit cairn			
Fountains Fell Tarn			
South top (662m) (869708)			

Notes _____

Times and Weather			
Departure time			
Arrival time			
Duration			
Weather			
Visibility			

Route details: # = via Yorkshire
Dales Cycle Way.

Gragareth   627m   2057'   NGR SD688793
Landranger 98   Outdoor Leisure 30

Route from				Ascent	Km	Time
Twistleton Lane (692760)				367	5.0	
Yorda's Cave				327	2.0	

Ridge routes				Descent	Ascent	Km
Green Hill				33	32	3.25

Features visited			
O.S. trig. point			
Cheese Press Stone			
Rowten Pot			
Three men of Gragareth			

Notes _____

Times and Weather			
Departure time			
Arrival time			
Duration			
Weather			
Visibility			

Great Coum   687m   2254'   NGR SD701836
Landranger 98   Outdoor Leisure 2

Route from				Ascent	Km	Time
Dent				537	5.5	

Ridge routes				Descent	Ascent	Km
Crag Hill				7	12	1.0
Green Hill				24	83	1.5
Whernside				271	222	6.0

Features visited				Notes _____
Summit				_____
Flinter Gill High Scout				_____
Megger Stones				_____
				_____

Times and Weather				_____
Departure time				_____
Arrival time				_____
Duration				_____
Weather				_____
Visibility				_____

Great Knoutberry Hill   672m   2205'   NGR SD788871
(Widdale Fell) Landranger 98   Outdoor Leisure 2

Route from				Ascent	Km	Time
Garside Station #				342	5.5	
Dent Station				322	3.0	
Stone House Bridge *				418	3.5	

Features visited				Notes _____
Summit cairn/stones				_____
O.S. trig. point				_____
Widdale Great Tarn				_____
Widdale Little Tarn				_____
Arten Gill Viaduct				_____
				_____

Times and Weather				_____
Departure time				_____
Arrival time				_____
Duration				Route details: # = via Galloway
Weather				Gate, * = via Arten Gill starting
Visibility				at G.R. 770859.

Great Shunner Fell   716m   2349' NGR SD849973
Landranger 98   Outdoor Leisure 30

Route from				Ascent	Km	Time
Buttertubs Pass (876956)				190	3.25	
Hardraw				478	7.0	
Thwaite				430	5.0	

Ridge routes				Descent	Ascent	Km
Hugh Seat				88	116	4.5
Little Fell				67	116	5.0
Lovely Seat				145	186	4.5

Features visited			
Summit stones			
O.S. trig. point			
Buttertubs			
Cairns above Fossdale Gill			
Little Shunner Fell (653m)			

Times and Weather			
Departure time			
Arrival time			
Duration			
Weather			
Visibility			

Notes _____
_____
_____
_____
_____
_____
_____
_____
_____
_____
_____
_____
_____
_____
_____
_____

Great Whernside   704m   2310'   NGR SE002739
Landranger 98   Outdoor Leisure 30

Route from/via				Ascent	Km	Time
Kettlewell via Hag Dyke				494	4.0	
Kettlewell #				494	4.0	
Starbottom				474	7.0	

Ridge routes				Descent	Ascent	Km
Buckden Pike				212	214	7.5
Tor Mere Top				417	204	5.0

Features visited			
Summit cairn			
O.S. trig. point			

Notes _____

_____

_____

_____

Times and Weather			
Departure time			
Arrival time			
Duration			
Weather			
Visibility			

_____

_____

_____

_____

Route details: # = via Dowber
Gill Beck.

Green Hill   628m   2060'   NGR SD702820
Landranger 98   Outdoor Leisure 2

Route from				Ascent	Km	Time

Ridge routes				Descent	Ascent	Km
Gragareth				32	33	3.25
Great Coum				83	24	1.5

Features visited			
Summit			

Notes _____

_____

_____

Times and Weather			
Departure time			
Arrival time			
Duration			
Weather			
Visibility			

_____

_____

_____

_____

_____

High Pike Hill   642m   2106'   NGR NY803032
Landranger 98

Route from				Ascent	Km	Time
Dalefoot				417	2.5	

Ridge routes				Descent	Ascent	Km
High Seat				74	17	2.0

Features visited				Notes _____
Summit				_____
				_____

Times and Weather				_____
Departure time				_____
Arrival time				_____
Duration				_____
Weather				_____
Visibility				_____

High Seat   709m   2326'   NGR NY802012
(Mallerstang Edge) Landranger 91

Route from				Ascent	Km	Time
Dalefoot				484	4.0	
Outhgill				449	2.0	

Ridge routes				Descent	Ascent	Km
Archy Styrigg				20	44	1.0
High Pike Hill				17	74	2.0

Features visited				Notes _____
Summit cairns				_____
				_____

Times and Weather				_____
Departure time				_____
Arrival time				_____
Duration				_____
Weather				_____
Visibility				_____

Hugh Seat   688m   2257'   NGR SD809991
Landranger 98

Route from				Ascent	Km	Time
Aisgill Moor Cottages #				324	5.0	

Ridge routes				Descent	Ascent	Km
Archy Styrigg				25	18	2.0
Great Shunner Fell				116	88	4.5
Little Fell				56	78	2.0

Features visited			
Summit cairn			
Lady's Pillar *			

Times and Weather			
Departure time			
Arrival time			
Duration			
Weather			
Visibility			

Notes _____

_____

_____

_____

_____

_____

_____

_____

_____

_____

_____

_____

_____

_____

Feature details: # = starts from G.R. 778963, * = in memory of Sir Hugh de Morville by Lady Anne Clifford (1664), rebuilt 1890.

Ingleborough   723m   2372'   NGR SD741746
Landranger 98   Outdoor Leisure 2

Route from			Ascent	Km	Time
Chapel-le-Dale			483	3.5	
Clapham			566	7.0	
Horton-in-Ribblesdale			488	7.0	
Ingleton			564	5.5	
Newby			570	5.5	

Ridge routes			Descent	Ascent	Km
Simon Fell			30	123	1.75

Features visited			
Summit cairn			
O.S. trig. point			
Summit windshelter			
Circular tower ruins (1830)			
Ingleborough Cave			
Gaping Gill (104m deep)			
Little Ingleborough (635m)			
Trow Gill			

Times and Weather			
Departure time			
Arrival time			
Duration			
Weather			
Visibility			

Notes _____

_____

_____

_____

_____

_____

_____

_____

_____

_____

_____

_____

_____

_____

_____

_____

Knoutberry Haw   676m   2218'   NGR SD731919
(Baugh Fell) Landranger 98   Outdoor Leisure 2

Route from				Ascent	Km	Time
A684 @ 694913				516	5.0	

Ridge routes				Descent	Ascent	Km
Baugh Fell (Tarn Rigg Hill)				21	23	1.0
Swarth Fell				295	290	6.0

Features visited				Notes _____
O.S. trig. point				

Times and Weather			
Departure time			
Arrival time			
Duration			
Weather			
Visibility			

Little Fell   667m   2188'   NGR SD808971
Landranger 98

Route from				Ascent	Km	Time
Aisgill Moor Cottages #				303	4.5	

Ridge routes				Descent	Ascent	Km
Great Shunner Fell				116	67	5.0
Hugh Seat				78	56	2.0
Sails				11	12	.75

Features visited				Notes _____
Summit cairn				
Hell Gill Force				

Times and Weather			
Departure time			
Arrival time			
Duration			
Weather			
Visibility			

Route details: # = starts from G.R. 778963.

Lovely Seat 675m 2215' NGR SD878951
Landranger 98 Outdoor Leisure 30

Route from				Ascent	Km	Time
Buttertubs Pass (867956)				149	1.25	
Hardraw				437	5.0+	

Ridge routes				Descent	Ascent	Km
Great Shunner Fell				186	145	4.5

Features visited			
Summit cairn			
Cliff Force			

Notes _____

Times and Weather			
Departure time			
Arrival time			
Duration			
Weather			
Visibility			

Nine Standards Rigg 662m 2172' NGR NY825061
Landranger 91 & 92

Route from				Ascent	Km	Time
Hartley				462	5.25	
Rowen Seat via pillar				362	6.5	
Rowen Seat #				362	6.0	
B6270 @ 809043				144	3.25	

Features visited			
Summit cairns (Nine Stds.)			
O.S. trig. point			

Notes _____

Times and Weather			
Departure time			
Arrival time			
Duration			
Weather			
Visibility			

Route details: # = via
Whitsundale Beck.

Pen-y-ghent   694m   2277'   NGR SD838734
Landranger 98   Outdoor Leisure 2

Route from				Ascent	Km	Time
Brackenbottom				374	2.5	
Horton-in-Ribblesdale				444	5.0	
Ribblehead				399	11.0	
Stainforth				494	7.0	

Ridge routes				Descent	Ascent	Km
Fountains Fell #				238	270	6.0
Plover Hill				60	74	2.5

Features visited			
Summit cairn			
O.S. trig. point			
Hull Pot			

Notes _____

Times and Weather			
Departure time			
Arrival time			
Duration			
Weather			
Visibility			

Route details: # = via Pennine Way.

Plover Hill   680m   2231'   NGR SD849752
Landranger 98   Outdoor Leisure 2

Route from				Ascent	Km	Time
Foxup #				372	3.5+	
Horton-in-Ribblesdale				448	5.5	

Ridge routes				Descent	Ascent	Km
Pen-y-ghent				74	60	2.5

Features visited			
Summit cairn			
Hull Pot			

Notes _____

Times and Weather			
Departure time			
Arrival time			
Duration			
Weather			
Visibility			

Route details: # = depending on route may be up to 9 Km.

Randygill Top   624m   2047'   NGR NY687001
Landranger 91

Route from				Ascent	Km	Time
Newbiggin-on-Lune				374	6.0	
Wath (686053)				394	5.75	

Ridge routes				Descent	Ascent	Km
Bush Howe				253	254	5.0
Yarlside				289	274	2.0

Features visited			
Summit cairn			

Times and Weather			
Departure time			
Arrival time			
Duration			
Weather			
Visibility			

Notes _____
_____
_____
_____
_____
_____
_____
_____
_____
_____

Rise Hill   556m   1824'   NGR SD721886
(Summit called Aye Gill Pike) Landranger 98

Route from				Ascent	Km	Time
Cawgill				333	5.0	
Dent				409	2.5	
Garsdale				177	4.5	

Features visited			
Summit cairn			
O.S. trig. point			

Times and Weather			
Departure time			
Arrival time			
Duration			
Weather			
Visibility			

Notes _____
_____
_____
_____
_____
_____
_____
_____
_____
_____

Rogan's Seat   672m   2205'   NGR NY919031
Landranger 91   Outdoor Leisure 30

Route from				Ascent	Km	Time
Gunnerside #				424	6.0	
Gunnerside *				424	10.0	
Muker				431	7.0	

Ridge routes				Descent	Ascent	Km
Water Crag				23	27	2.0

Features visited				Notes _____
Summit cairn				
Shooting box (907027)				

Times and Weather			
Departure time			
Arrival time			
Duration			
Weather			
Visibility			

Route details: # = via Jingle Pot Edge, * = via Ivelet Side.

Sails   666m   2185'   NGR SD808965
Landranger 98

Route from				Ascent	Km	Time
Aisgill Moor Cottages #				302	4.0	

Ridge routes				Descent	Ascent	Km
Little Fell				12	11	.75

Features visited				Notes _____
Summit				

Times and Weather			
Departure time			
Arrival time			
Duration			
Weather			
Visibility			

Route details: # = starts from G.R. 778963

Simon Fell   650m   2133'   SD755752

Landranger 98   Outdoor Leisure 2

Route from				Ascent	Km	Time
Chapel-le-Dale				410	3.75	
Horton-in-Ribblesdale				415	6.25	

Ridge routes				Descent	Ascent	Km
Ingleborough				123	30	1.75

Features visited			
Summit stones			

Times and Weather			
Departure time			
Arrival time			
Duration			
Weather			
Visibility			

Notes _____

Swarth Fell   681m   2234'   NGR SD756967

Landranger 98

Route from				Ascent	Km	Time
Aisgill Moor Cottages #				317	3.0	

Ridge routes				Descent	Ascent	Km
Baugh Fell				378	381	6.0
Knoutberry Haw				290	295	6.0
Wild Boar Fell				103	76	2.5

Features visited			
Summit cairn			
Swarth Fell Pike (761958)			

Times and Weather			
Departure time			
Arrival time			
Duration			
Weather			
Visibility			

Notes _____

Route details: # = starts from
G.R. 778963.

Tor Mere Top   617m   2024'   NGR SD970765
Landranger 98   Outdoor Leisure 30

Route from/via			Ascent	Km	Time
Kettlewell			407	5.0	
Starbottom/Walden Road			394	5.5	
Starbottom via Cam Row			394	3.0	

Ridge routes			Descent	Ascent	Km
Buckden Pike			87	12	2.75
Great Whernside			204	417	5.0

Features visited				Notes _____
Summit				_____
				_____

Times and Weather				_____
Departure time				_____
Arrival time				_____
Duration				_____
Weather				_____
Visibility				_____

Water Crag   668m   2192'   NGR NY928046
Landranger 91   Outdoor Leisure 30

Route from			Ascent	Km	Time
Gunnerside			420	8.0	
Langthwaite			405	9.0	

Ridge routes			Descent	Ascent	Km
Rogan's Seat			27	23	2.0

Features visited				Notes _____
O.S. trig. point				_____
windshelter				_____
				_____

Times and Weather				_____
Departure time				_____
Arrival time				_____
Duration				_____
Weather				_____
Visibility				_____

Whernside   736m   2415'   NGR SD738814
Landranger 98   Outdoor Leisure 2

Route from				Ascent	Km	Time
Chapel-le-Dale				496	4.0	
Dent via Craven Way				586	9.0	
Dent via Deepdale				586	8.0	
Dent via Occupation Road				586	10.0	
Ingleton				577	9.5	
Ribblehead				441	4.0	

Ridge routes				Descent	Ascent	Km
Great Coum				222	271	6.0

Features visited			
Summit cairn			
O.S. trig. point			
Thornton Force (12m)			
Pecca Falls			
Greensett Tarns			
Whernside Tarns			

Times and Weather			
Departure time			
Arrival time			
Duration			
Weather			
Visibility			

Notes _____

_____

_____

_____

_____

_____

_____

_____

_____

_____

_____

_____

_____

_____

_____

Wild Boar Fell   708m   2323'   NGR SD758988
Landranger 98

Route from				Ascent	Km	Time
Aisgill Moor Cottages #				344	4.5	

Ridge routes				Descent	Ascent	Km
Swarth Fell				76	103	2.5

Features visited			
Summit cairn			
O.S. trig. point			
Angerholme Pots			

Notes _____
_____
_____
_____
_____
_____

Times and Weather			
Departure time			
Arrival time			
Duration			
Weather			
Visibility			

Route details: # = starts from
G.R. 778963.

Yarlside   639m   2097'   NGR SD686985
Landranger 98

Route from				Ascent	Km	Time
Low Haygarth (697967)				449	3.0	

Ridge routes				Descent	Ascent	Km
The Calf				256	219	3.0
Randygill Top				274	289	2.0

Features visited			
Summit cairn			
Cautley Spout			

Notes _____

Times and Weather			
Departure time			
Arrival time			
Duration			
Weather			
Visibility			

Yockenthwaite Moor   643m   2110'   NGR SD909811
Landranger 98 Outdoor Leisure 39

Route from				Ascent	Km	Time
Gilbert Lane (943803)				224	4.5	
Hubberholme				403	3.5	
Yockenthwaite				423	3.5	

Features visited			
O.S. trig. point			
Middle Tongue Tarn			

Times and Weather			
Departure time			
Arrival time			
Duration			
Weather			
Visibility			

Notes

CHAPTER FOUR

PEAK DISTRICT and DARTMOOR

Mountain	Page	Height in Metres	Date first Ascended
Peak District			
Back Tor	67	538	___:___:___
Black Hill	67	582	___:___:___
Bleaklow Head	68	633	___:___:___
Brown Knoll	69	569	___:___:___
Higher Shelf Stones	69	621	___:___:___
High Neb	70	458	___:___:___
Kinder Scout	71	636	___:___:___
Lord's Seat	72	550	___:___:___
Mam Tor	72	517	___:___:___
Margery Hill	73	546	___:___:___
Mill Hill	73	544	___:___:___
Dartmoor			
High Willhays	74	621	___:___:___
Yes Tor	74	619	___:___:___

PEAK DISTRICT

Back Tor   538m 1765' NGR SK198910
Landranger 110   Outdoor Leisure 1

Route from				Ascent	Km	Time
National Park Centre #				328	4.5	
Strines Reservoir (222905)				218	3.0	
					.	

Ridge routes				Descent	Ascent	Km
Margery Hill				71	63	5.75

Features visited				Notes _____
Summit cairn				_____
O.S. trig. point				_____
Cakes of Bread				_____
				_____

Times and Weather				_____
Departure time				_____
Arrival time				_____
Duration				_____
Weather				Route details: # = from
Visibility				G.R.172893.

Black Hill   582m   1909' NGR SK078047
(Soldier's Lump) Landranger 110   Outdoor Leisure 1

Route from				Ascent	Km	Time
Crowden #				365	7.25	
Crowden *				365	6.0	

Features visited				Notes _____
Summit cairn				_____
O.S. trig. point				_____
Laddow Rocks				_____
				_____

Times and Weather				_____
Departure time				_____
Arrival time				_____
Duration				Route details: # = via Pennine
Weather				Way, * = via White Law
Visibility				(Westend Moss).

Bleaklow Head   633m   2077'   NGR SK092959
Landranger 110   Outdoor Leisure 1

Route from/via				Ascent	Km	Time
Crowden				423	8.25	
Nat. Park Centre (068984)				433	5.5	
Old Glossop/Doctor's Gate				463	8.5	
Old Glossop/Cock Hill				463	6.5	
Snake Pass A57 (088929)				121	4.0	

Ridge routes				Descent	Ascent	Km
Higher Shelf Stones				15	27	1.25

Features visited			
Summit cairn			
Devils Dyke			
Bleaklow Stones			
Hern Stones			
Wain Stones			

Times and Weather			
Departure time			
Arrival time			
Duration			
Weather			
Visibility			

Notes _____

_____

_____

_____

_____

_____

_____

_____

_____

_____

_____

_____

_____

_____

Brown Knoll 569m 1867' NGR SK084852
Landranger 110 Outdoor Leisure 1

Route from				Ascent	Km	Time
Barber Booth (107847)				309	4.0c	
Upper Booth				299	4.5c	

Ridge routes				Descent	Ascent	Km
Kinder Scout				103	36	3.25
Lord's Seat				62	81	4.0

Features visited				Notes
Summit cairn				
O.S. trig. point				

Times and Weather			
Departure time			
Arrival time			
Duration			
Weather			
Visibility			

Higher Shelf Stones 621m 2038' NGR SK089948
Landranger 110 Outdoor Leisure 1

Route from				Ascent	Km	Time
Old Glossop #				421	6.75	
Old Glossop *				421	8.25	
Snake Pass A57 (088929)				109	3.25	

Ridge routes				Descent	Ascent	Km
Bleaklow Head				27	15	1.25

Features visited				Notes
Summit cairn				
O.S. trig. point				
Devils Dyke				
Super Fortress wreckage				

Times and Weather			
Departure time			
Arrival time			
Duration			
Weather			
Visibility			

Route details: # = via Doctor's Gate and Crooked Clough, * = via Doctor's Gate and Pennine Way.

High Neb   458m   1502'   NGR SK228853
(Stanage Edge) Landranger 110

Route from				Ascent	Km	Time
Hathersage (232815)				279	5.0	
Ladybower Res'r. (204864)				288	5.5	

Features visited			
Summit cairn			
O.S. trig. point			

Times and Weather			
Departure time			
Arrival time			
Duration			
Weather			
Visibility			

Notes _____
_____
_____
_____
_____
_____
_____
_____
_____
_____
_____
_____
_____
_____

Kinder Scout   636m   2088'   NGR SK085875
Landranger 110   Outdoor Leisure 1

Route from/via				Ascent	Km	Time
Barber Booth (107847)				361	5.75	
Edale/Crowden Brook				396	6.5	
Edale/Golden Clough				396	7.5	
Edale/Grindsbook Clough				396	5.75	
Edale/Ollerbrook Clough				396	8.0	
Edale/Pennine Way #				396	7.75	

Ridge routes				Descent	Ascent	Km
Brown Knoll				36	103	3.25
Mill Hill				nil	36	6.0

Other Kinder summits/tops visited				Grid Ref.
Crowden Head (632m)				096881
Grindslow Knoll (601m)				110868
Hartshorn (604m)				115877
Kinder Low (633m)				079871

Features visited			
Summit cairn			
Edale Cross			
Jacob's Ladder			
Pym Chair			

Times and Weather			
Departure time			
Arrival time			
Duration			
Weather			
Visibility			

Notes _____

_____

_____

_____

_____

_____

_____

_____

_____

_____

Route details: # = via Pennine Way and Edale Cross.

Lord's Seat   550m   1805'   NGR SK112834
Landranger 110   Outdoor Leisure 1

Route from				Ascent	Km	Time
Barber Booth (107847) #				290	4.25	
Speedwell Cavern *				300	3.25	
A625 picnic area (122832)				130	1.75	

Ridge routes				Descent	Ascent	Km
Brown Knoll				81	62	4.0
Mam Tor				62	95	1.5

Features visited			
Summit cairn			

Notes _____

Times and Weather			
Departure time			
Arrival time			
Duration			
Weather			
Visibility			

Route details: # = via Chapel Gate, * = via Winnats Pass.

Mam Tor   517m   1696'   NGR SK128836
Landranger 110   Outdoor Leisure 1

Route from				Ascent	Km	Time
Barber Booth (107847)				257	3.25	
Castleton #				327	3.75	
Edale				277	2.25	
Speedwell Cavern *				267	2.5	
A625 picnic area (122832)				97	.75	

Ridge routes				Descent	Ascent	Km
Lord's Seat				95	62	1.5

Features visited			
Summit cairn			
O.S. trig. point			
Iron age fort			

Notes _____

Times and Weather			
Departure time			
Arrival time			
Duration			
Weather			
Visibility			

Route details: # = via Hollins Cross, * = via Winnats Pass.

Margery Hill   546m   1791'   NGR SK189957
Landranger 110   Outdoor Leisure 1

Route from				Ascent	Km	Time
Flouch Inn (197015)				265	6.5	
Langsett				296	7.5	
National Park Centre #				336	7.5	

Ridge routes				Descent	Ascent	Km
Back Tor				63	71	5.75

Features visited			
Summit cairn			
O.S. trig. point			
Margery Stones			

Times and Weather			
Departure time			
Arrival time			
Duration			
Weather			
Visibility			

Notes _____

_____

_____

_____

_____

_____

_____

_____

Route details: # = from
Ladybower National Park
Centre @ G.R. 172893.

Mill Hill   544m   1785'   NGR SK061904
Landranger 110   Outdoor Leisure 1

Route from				Ascent	Km	Time
Hayfield Visitor Centre				344	5.0	
Hollingworth Head Farm #				214	2.75	

Ridge routes				Descent	Ascent	Km
Kinder Scout				36	nil	6.0

Features visited			
Summit cairn			

Times and Weather			
Departure time			
Arrival time			
Duration			
Weather			
Visibility			

Notes _____

_____

_____

_____

_____

_____

_____

Route details: # = from G. R.
033903.

DARTMOOR

High Willhays   621m   2038'   NGR SY580893
Landranger 191   Outdoor Leisure 28

Route from				Ascent	Km	Time
Meldon Reservoir (562919)				341	4.0	

Ridge routes				Descent	Ascent	Km
Yes Tor				24	26	1.25

Features visited			
Summit cairn			

Times and Weather			
Departure time			
Arrival time			
Duration			
Weather			
Visibility			

Notes _____

Yes Tor   619m   2031'   NGR SX581902
Landranger 191   Outdoor Leisure 28

Route from				Ascent	Km	Time
Meldon Reservoir (562919)				339	3.25	

Ridge routes				Descent	Ascent	Km
High Willhays				26	24	1.25

Features visited			
O.S. trig. point			

Times and Weather			
Departure time			
Arrival time			
Duration			
Weather			
Visibility			

Notes _____

CHAPTER FIVE

NORTHERN LAKE DISTRICT

Mountain	Page	Height in Metres	Date first Ascended
Bakestall	76	673	__:__:__
Bannerdale Crags	76	683	__:__:__
Binsey	77	447	__:__:__
Blencathra	78	868	28:08:00
Bowscale Fell	80	702	__:__:__
Brae Fell	81	585	__:__:__
Carl Side	81	746	4:9:00
Carrock Fell	82	660	__:__:__
Dodd	82	502	__:__:__
Great Calva	83	690	__:__:__
Great Cockup	83	526	__:__:__
Great Lingy Hill	84	616	__:__:__
Great Sca Fell	84	651	__:__:__
High Pike	75	658	__:__:__
Knott	86	710	__:__:__
Latrigg	86	367	__:__:__
Little Calva	87	642	__:__:__
Longlands Fell	87	482	__:__:__
Long Side	88	734	4:9:00
Lonscale Fell	88	715	__:__:__
Meal Fell	89	540	__:__:__
Mungrisdale Common	89	633	__:__:__
Sale How	90	666	__:__:__
Skiddaw	91	931	04:09:00
Skiddaw Little Man	92	865	__:__:__
Souther Fell	92	522	__:__:__
Ullock Pike	93	680	04:09:00

Bakestall   673m   2208'   NGR NY266307
Landranger 89 & 90

Route from				Ascent	Km	Time
Bassenthwaite Village				573	4.75	
High Side				545	5.0	
Skiddaw House				203	3.25	

Ridge routes				Descent	Ascent	Km
Skiddaw				266	8	1.75

Features visited				Notes_____
Summit cairn				_____
Whitewater Dash Falls				_____
				_____

Times and Weather				_____
Departure time				_____
Arrival time				_____
Duration				_____
Weather				_____
Visibility				_____

Bannerdale Crags   683m   2241'   NGR NY335290
Landranger 90   Outdoor Leisure 5

Route from				Ascent	Km	Time
Mungrisdale #				463	4.5	
Mungrisdale *				463	4.75	
Scales 1				458	4.5	
Scales 2				458	3.5	

Ridge routes				Descent	Ascent	Km
Blencathra				243	58	2.25
Bowscale Fell				57	38	2.0
Mungrisdale Common				8	58	2.5

Features visited				Notes_____
Summit cairn				_____
Bannerdale Lead Mine				_____
				_____

Times and Weather				_____
Departure time				Route details: # = via The
Arrival time				Tongue, * = via River
Duration				Glenderamackin, 1 = via River
Weather				Glenderamackin and col @
Visibility				328291, 2 = via White Horse
				Bent.

Binsey 447m 1467' NGR NY225355
Landranger 89 & 90

Route from				Ascent	Km	Time
Bewaldeth & Fell End				277	2.0	
Fell End (222348)				227	1.0	
High Bewaldeth				262	1.5	
High Houses (217327)				247	1.75	
High Ireby				247	2.0	

Features visited			
Summit cairn			
O.S. trig. point			
Summit tumulus			

Times and Weather			
Departure time			
Arrival time			
Duration			
Weather			
Visibility			

Notes_____
_____
_____
_____
_____
_____
_____
_____
_____
_____
_____
_____
_____
_____
_____
_____
_____
_____

Blencathra (1)   868m   2848'   NGR NY323277
Landranger 90   Outdoor Leisure 4 & 5

Route from	3-9-00			Ascent	Km	Time
Blencathra Centre #				598	3.25	
Blencathra Centre *				598	4.25	
Scales via Doddick Fell	DESCENT			643	2.75	
Scales via Halls Fell				643	2.5	
Scales via Scaley Beck				643	2.5	
Scales via Scales Fell				643	3.25	
Scales via Sharp Edge	ASCENT			643	4.0	

Features visited			
Summit cairn (Hallsfell top)	NO		
Gategill Fell Top (851m)	NO		
Atkinson Pike (845m)	YES		
White (Robinson) Cross	YES		
Smaller white cross	NO		
Sharp Edge	YES		
Scales Tarn	YES		
Gategill Mine	NO		
Glenderaterra Mine	NO		

Times and Weather			
Departure time	10:51AM		
Arrival time	12:25PM		
Duration	1H34M		
Weather	Cool Sunny		
Visibility	Good		

Notes_____

Route details: # = via Blease Fell, * = via Roughten Gill.

Blencathra (2)

Route from Threlkeld	28-8-00			Ascent	Km	Time
via Blease Gill	DESCENT			668	2.5	
via Doddick Fell (328258)				688	3.0	
via Gategill Fell				688	2.5	
via Gategill & #				688	2.5	
via Halls Fell (328258)	ASCENT			688	2.0	

Ridge routes			Descent	Ascent	Km
Bannerdale Crags			58	243	2.25
Bowscale Fell			77	243	3.0
Mungrisdale Common			8	243	2.0

Features visited			
Summit cairn (Hallsfell top)	YES		
Gategill Fell Top (851m)	YES		
Atkinson Pike (845m)	NO		
White (Robinson) Cross	NO		
Smaller white cross	NO		
Sharp Edge	NO		
Scales Tarn	NO		
Gategill Mine	NO		
Glenderaterra Mine	NO		

Times and Weather			
Departure time	10:00 AM		
Arrival time	11:35 AM		
Duration	1HR 35 min		
Weather			
Visibility	V. GOOD		

Notes_____

_____
_____
_____
_____
_____
_____
_____
_____
_____
_____
_____

Route details: # = via Gategill and Middle Tongue at G.R. 328258.

Bowscale Fell   702m   2303'   NGR NY333305
Landranger 90

Route from/via				Ascent	Km	Time
Bowscale/Bowscale Tarn				462	3.5	
Bowscale via East ridge				462	2.75	
Mungrisdale via:						
Bullfell Beck				462	3.0	
East ridge				462	3.25	
The Tongue				462	3.0	
main path #				462	3.25	

Ridge routes				Descent	Ascent	Km
Bannerdale Crags				38	57	2.0
Blencathra				243	77	3.0
Mungrisdale Common				8	77	3.25

Features visited			
Summit windshelter			
Subsidiary summit (671m)			
Bowscale Tarn			

Times and Weather			
Departure time			
Arrival time			
Duration			
Weather			
Visibility			

Notes_____
_____
_____
_____
_____
_____
_____
_____
_____
_____
_____
_____
_____
_____
_____

Brae Fell 585m 1919' NGR NY289352
Landranger 89 & 90

Route from			Ascent	Km	Time
Branthwaite (299374)			335	2.75	
Greenhead (286371)			331	2.0	
Fell Side (306375)			335	3.75	
Longlands (267359)			355	4.0	

Ridge routes			Descent	Ascent	Km
Great Sca Fell			66	10	1.25

Features visited			
Summit cairn			

Times and Weather			
Departure time			
Arrival time			
Duration			
Weather			
Visibility			

Notes_____

_____
_____
_____
_____
_____
_____
_____
_____

Carl Side 746m 2448' NGR NY255281
Landranger 89 & 90 Outdoor Leisure 4

Route from	4-9-00		Ascent	Km	Time
Dodd Wood c.p. (235281)			636	2.75	
High Side via Southerndale			596	4.25	
Little Crosthwaite (234276)			646	3.0	
Millbeck			621	2.0	

Ridge routes			Descent	Ascent	Km
Dodd			102	346	1.5
Long Side #	P.88	FROM	9+	21+	.75
Skiddaw	P.91	ONTO	216	31	1.5
Skiddaw Little Man			150	31	1.75

Features visited			
Summit cairn	✳	NO	

Times and Weather			
Departure time	12:15		
Arrival time	12:25		
Duration	10 MINS		
Weather	SUNNY		
Visibility	V. GOOD		

Notes We didn't Summit but walked the Northern flank @ 715 metres above sea-level.

Route details: # = the ridge between summits is higher than the summits themselves @ 755m.

Carrock Fell   660m   2165'   NGR NY342336
Landranger 90

Route from				Ascent	Km	Time
Calebreck				360	4.5	
Mosedale				420	2.0	
Stone Ends Farm (355335)				440	1.25	

Ridge routes				Descent	Ascent	Km
Great Lingy Hill				41	85	3.0
High Pike				83	85	3.25

Features visited				Notes
Summit cairn				
Miton Hill				
Iron age hill fort				
Carrock Mine				

Times and Weather			
Departure time			
Arrival time			
Duration			
Weather			
Visibility			

Dodd   502m   1647'   NGR NY244274
Landranger 89 & 90   Outdoor Leisure 4

Route from				Ascent	Km	Time
Dodd Wood c. p. (235281)				392	1.5	
Little Crosthwaite (234276)				402	2.0c	
Millbeck				377	2.0	

Ridge routes				Descent	Ascent	Km
Carl Side				346	102	1.5

Features visited				Notes
Summit cairn				

Times and Weather			
Departure time			
Arrival time			
Duration			
Weather			
Visibility			

Great Calva   690m   2264'   NGR NY291312
Landranger 89 & 90

Route from				Ascent	Km	Time
Bassenthwaite				590	7.0c	
Mosedale				450	7.75c	
Orthwaite				452	6.5c	
Skiddaw House				220	2.5	

Ridge routes				Descent	Ascent	Km
Knott				155	135	2.5
Little Calva				17	65	1.0

Features visited			
Summit cairn			
Summit windshelter			
Whitewater Dash Falls			

Notes_____
_____
_____
_____
_____
_____
_____

Times and Weather			
Departure time			
Arrival time			
Duration			
Weather			
Visibility			

Great Cockup   526m   1726'   NGR NY273334
Landranger 89 & 90

Route from				Ascent	Km	Time
Longlands				296	3.5	
Orthwaite via South path				288	3.0	
Orthwaite via Trusmadoor				288	3.75	

Ridge routes				Descent	Ascent	Km
Meal Fell				105	91	1.0

Features visited			
Summit cairn			

Notes_____
_____
_____

Times and Weather			
Departure time			
Arrival time			
Duration			
Weather			
Visibility			

Great Lingy Hill   616m   2021'   NGR NY310340
Landranger 90

Route from				Ascent	Km	Time
Mosedale				376	5.25	

Ridge routes				Descent	Ascent	Km
Carrock Fell				85	41	3.0
High Pike				63	21	1.25
Knott				125	31	2.0

Features visited			
Summit cairn			

Times and Weather			
Departure time			
Arrival time			
Duration			
Weather			
Visibility			

Notes_____
_____
_____
_____
_____
_____
_____
_____
_____
_____
_____

Great Sca Fell   651m   2136'   NGR NY291339
Landranger 89 & 90

Route from				Ascent	Km	Time
Fell Side				366	4.0	
Greenhead (286371)				397	4.75	
Longlands (267359)				421	4.25	
Orthwaite				413	5.0	

Ridge routes				Descent	Ascent	Km
Brae Fell				10	66	1.25
Longlands Fell				37	206	2.5
Meal Fell				65	176	1.0
Knott				75	16	1.25

Features visited			
Summit			

Times and Weather			
Departure time			
Arrival time			
Duration			
Weather			
Visibility			

Notes_____
_____
_____
_____
_____
_____
_____
_____
_____
_____

High Pike   658m   2159'   NGR NY319350
Landranger 90

Route from				Ascent	Km	Time
Calebreck				358	3.75	
Fell Side				373	4.5	
Nether Row				388	3.25	
Hesket Newmarket				488	5.0	

Ridge routes				Descent	Ascent	Km
Carrock Fell				85	83	3.25
Great Lingy Hill				21	63	1.25

Features visited			
Summit cairn			
O.S. trig. point			
Various mines			
Slate memorial seat			

Times and Weather			
Departure time			
Arrival time			
Duration			
Weather			
Visibility			

Notes_____
_____
_____
_____
_____
_____
_____
_____
_____
_____
_____
_____
_____
_____

Knott   710m   2330'   NGR NY296330
Landranger 89 & 90

Route from				Ascent	Km	Time
Fell Side				425	5.0	
Longlands Fell				480	5.0	
Mosedale				470	6.25	
Orthwaite				472	5.0	

Ridge routes				Descent	Ascent	Km
Great Calva				135	155	2.5
Great Lingy Hill				31	125	2.0
Great Sca Fell				16	75	1.25
Little Calva				87	155	2.0

Features visited			
Summit cairn			

Times and Weather			
Departure time			
Arrival time			
Duration			
Weather			
Visibility			

Notes_____
_____
_____
_____
_____
_____
_____
_____
_____
_____

Latrigg   367m   1207'   NGR NY278247
Landranger 89 & 90   Outdoor Leisure 4

Route from				Ascent	Km	Time
Keswick @ 269240				263	2.5	
car park @ 281253				27	1.5	

Features visited			
Summit			

Times and Weather			
Departure time			
Arrival time			
Duration			
Weather			
Visibility			

Notes_____
_____
_____
_____
_____
_____
_____
_____
_____

Little Calva 642m 2106' NGR NY282315
Landranger 89 & 90

Route from				Ascent	Km	Time
Bassenthwaite				542	6.5	
Mosedale				402	9.0c	
Orthwaite				404	6.25	
Skiddaw House				172	2.75	

Ridge routes				Descent	Ascent	Km
Great Calva				65	17	1.0
Knott				155	87	2.0

Features visited				Notes
Summit stones/cairn				
Whitewater Dash Falls				

Times and Weather			
Departure time			
Arrival time			
Duration			
Weather			
Visibility			

Longlands Fell 482m 1581' NGR NY276354
Landranger 89 & 90

Route from				Ascent	Km	Time
Longlands				182	1.5	
Orthwaite				244	4.0	

Ridge routes				Descent	Ascent	Km
Great Sca Fell				206	37	2.5

Features visited				Notes
Summit cairn				
Lowthwaite Fell				

Times and Weather			
Departure time			
Arrival time			
Duration			
Weather			
Visibility			

Long Side   734m   2408'   NGR NY249284
Landranger 89 & 90   Outdoor Leisure 4

Route from	4-9-00			Ascent	Km	Time
Dodd Wood c.p. (235281)				624	3.25c	
Little Crosthwaite (234276)				634	3.5c	
Millbeck				609	2.75	

Ridge routes				Descent	Ascent	Km
Carl Side #	P-81	ONTO		21+	1+	.75
Ullock Pike	P.93	FROM		nil	54	.5

Features visited			
Summit cairn	YES		

Times and Weather			
Departure time	12:00		
Arrival time	12:15		
Duration	15 MINS		
Weather	SUNNY		
Visibility	V.GOOD		

Notes_____

Route details: # = the ridge
between summits is higher than
the summits themselves @
755m.

Lonscale Fell   715m   2346'   NGR NY285271
Landranger 89 & 90   Outdoor Leisure 4

Route from				Ascent	Km	Time
Blencathra Centre				445	3.75c	
Latrigg car park (281253)				320	3.5c	
Threlkeld				525	5.5	

Ridge routes				Descent	Ascent	Km
Sale How				161	210	1.75
Skiddaw Little Man				200	50	2.0

Features visited			
Summit cairn			

Times and Weather			
Departure time			
Arrival time			
Duration			
Weather			
Visibility			

Notes_____

Meal Fell   540m   1772' NGR NY238388
Landranger 89 & 90

Route from				Ascent	Km	Time
Longlands				310	3.0	
Orthwaite via Trusmadoor				302	4.0	
Orthwaite avoiding Trusmadoor				302	3.75	

Ridge routes				Descent	Ascent	Km
Great Cockup				91	105	1.0
Great Sca Fell				176	65	1.0

Features visited				Notes_____
Summit/shelter				

Times and Weather			
Departure time			
Arrival time			
Duration			
Weather			
Visibility			

Mungrisdale Common   633m   2077' NGR NY312294
Landranger 90   Outdoor Leisure 4 & 5

Route from				Ascent	Km	Time
Mungrisdale				413	7.0	
Scales				408	5.0	

Ridge routes				Descent	Ascent	Km
Bannerdale Crags				58	8	2.5
Blencathra				243	8	2.0
Bowscale Fell				77	8	3.25

Features visited				Notes_____
Summit cairn				
Cloven Stone				

Times and Weather			
Departure time			
Arrival time			
Duration			
Weather			
Visibility			

Sale How   666m   2185'   NGR NY276286
Landranger 90   Outdoor Leisure 4

Route from				Ascent	Km	Time
Bassenthwaite				566	8.25	
Melbecks				496	6.75	
Mosedale				426	9.5	
Orthwaite				428	8.0	
Skiddaw House				206	1.25	

Ridge routes				Descent	Ascent	Km
Lonscale Fell				210	161	1.75
Skiddaw House				336	71	1.75
Skiddaw Little Man				270	71	1.25

Features visited			
Summit cairn			

Times and Weather			
Departure time			
Arrival time			
Duration			
Weather			
Visibility			

Notes_____
_____
_____
_____
_____
_____
_____
_____
_____
_____
_____
_____
_____
_____
_____

Skiddaw   931m   3054' NGR NY260291

Landranger 89 & 90   Outdoor Leisure 4

Route from	4-9-00			Ascent	Km	Time
Bassenthwaite				831	3.0	
Dodd Wood c.p. (235281) #				821	4.0	
Latrigg car park				535	4.75	
Melbecks				751	1.75	
Millbeck #				806	3.25	
Keswick				830c	6.7- 8.5c	
Ravenstone (235296)	DESCENT					

Ridge routes				Descent	Ascent	Km
Bakestall				8	266	1.75
Carl Side	FROM			31	216	1.5
Sale How				71	336	1.75
Skiddaw Little Man				60	126	1.5

Features visited			
Summit cairns	YES		
O.S. trig. point	YES		
Topograph	YES		
Windshelter	YES		
North top (831m)	YES		
South top (928m)	YES		
WATCH STONES	DESCENT		

Times and Weather			
Departure time	12:25		
Arrival time	13:05		
Duration	40 MINS		
Weather	SUNNY		
Visibility	GOOD		

Notes Bleak mountain - not in a hurry to climb this one again !!

Route details: # = via Carl Side summit.

Skiddaw Little Man   865m   2838'   NGR NY267278
Landranger 90   Outdoor Leisure 4

Route from				Ascent	Km	Time
Applethwaite via Howgill				727	2.75	
Millbeck, direct				740	2.5	
Millbeck via Carl Side *				740	4.0	
Millbeck via Slade Beck				740	4.0	
Skiddaw House #				395	2.75	

Ridge routes				Descent	Ascent	Km
Carl Side (see * above)				31	150	1.75
Lonscale Fell				50	200	2.0
Sale How				71	270	1.25
Skiddaw				126	60	1.5

Features visited			
Summit cairn			

Times and Weather			
Departure time			
Arrival time			
Duration			
Weather			
Visibility			

Notes_____

_____

_____

_____

_____

_____

_____

_____

_____

Route details: # = skirting Sale How.

Souther Fell   522m   1713'   NGR NY355291
Landranger 90   Outdoor Leisure 5

Route from				Ascent	Km	Time
Mungrisdale				302	2.0	
Scales				297	3.0	

Features visited			
Summit cairn			

Times and Weather			
Departure time			
Arrival time			
Duration			
Weather			
Visibility			

Notes_____

_____

_____

_____

_____

_____

_____

_____

Ullock Pike   680m   2231'   NGR NY244287
Landranger 89 & 90   Outdoor Leisure 4

Route from	4-9-00			Ascent	Km	Time
Bassenthwaite				580	2.25	
Dodd Wood c.p. (235281)				570	1.25	
High Side				552	1.75	
Ravenstone (235296)	ASCENT			576	2.25	

Ridge routes				Descent	Ascent	Km
Long Side P.88	ONTO			54	nil	.5

Features visited			
Summit cairn	YES		

Times and Weather			
Departure time	10:45		
Arrival time	12:00		
Duration	1H15M		
Weather	SUNNY		
Visibility	GOOD		

Notes_____
_____
_____
_____
_____
_____
_____
_____
_____
_____
_____
_____
_____
_____

CHAPTER SIX

EASTERN LAKE DISTRICT

Mountain	Page	Height in Metres	Date first Ascended
Arnison Crag	95	433	9 - 9 07
Birkhouse Moor	95	718	10 . 9 . 97
Birks	96	622	2 . 5 . 05
Catstye Cam	96	890	7 . 9 . 07
Clough Head	97	726	__ : __ : __
Dollywaggon Pike	97	858	6 : 5 : 05
Dove Crag	98	792	? : 09 : 96
Fairfield	98	873	? : 09 : 96
Glenridding Dodd	99	442	2 . 9 . 07
Gowbarrow Fell	99	481	__ : __ : __
Great Dodd	100	857	__ : __ : __
Great Mell Fell	100	537	__ : __ : __
Great Rigg (inc.Stone Arthur)	101	766	? : 09 : 96
Green Side	101	795	__ : __ : __
Hart Crag	102	822	? : 09 : 96
Hart Side	102	756	__ : __ : __
Hartsop-above-How	103	570	2 . 5 . 02
Helvellyn	104/5	950	10 . 09 . 97 (Malc - Sep'9
Helvellyn Lower Man	106	925	__ : __ : __
Heron Pike	107	612	? : 09 : 96
High Hartsop Dodd	107	519	__ : __ : __
High Pike	108	656	? : 09 : 96
Little Hart Crag	109	637	__ : __ : __
Little Mell Fell	110	505	__ : __ : __
Low Pike	110	508	? : 09 : 96
Middle Dodd	111	654	__ : __ : __
Nab Scar	111	445	? : 09 : 96
Nethermost Pike	112	891	6 : 5 : 05
Raise	113	883	__ : __ : __
Red Screes	114	776	__ : __ : __
Saint Sunday Crag	115	841	2 . 5 . 05
Seat Sandal	115	736	6 . 5 . 05
Sheffield Pike	116	675	2 . 9 . 07
Stybarrow Dodd	116	843	__ : __ : __
Watson's Dodd	117	789	__ : __ : __
White Side	117	863	__ : __ : __

Arnison Crag   433m   1906'   NGR NY394149
Landranger 90   Outdoor Leisure 5

Route from	9-9-07			Ascent	Km	Time
Patterdale				283	1.25c	

Ridge routes				Descent	Ascent	Km
Birks				207	18	1.75
St. Sunday Crag				426	18	3.25

Features visited			
Summit cairn	YES		

Notes _____
_____

Times and Weather			
Departure time			
Arrival time			
Duration			
Weather	DULL, DRY		
Visibility	GOOD		

Birkhouse Moor   718m   2356'   NGR NY363160
Landranger 90   Outdoor Leisure 5

Route from	10-9-97	7-9-07		Ascent	Km	Time
Glenridding Via Lanty's Tarn	DESCENT			558	2.5	
Patterdale (396159)				568	3.5	
GLENRIDDING (Mires Beck)	-	ASCENT				

Ridge routes				Descent	Ascent	Km
Catstye Cam				195	23	2.25
Helvellyn via Striding Edge P.105		ONTO		255	23	3.0
Helvellyn via Swirral Edge P.105	FROM			255	23	2.75

Features visited			
Summit cairn ✗	NO	YES	
North East cairn	NO	NO	
Keldas	NO	NO	
Lanty's Tarn	YES	NO	

Notes We didn't
Summit but walked
the Southern flank
in 1997.
_____
_____

Times and Weather			
Departure time	?		
Arrival time	?		
Duration	?		
Weather	HOT SUNNY	HOT SUNNY	
Visibility	V. GOOD	V GOOD	

Birks   622m   2041'   NGR NY380144
Landranger 90   Outdoor Leisure 5

Route from	2505			Ascent	Km	Time
Patterdale (396159)	ASCENT			472	2.75c	

Ridge routes				Descent	Ascent	Km
Arnison Crag				18	207	1.75
St. Sunday Crag	ONTO			238	19	1.5

Features visited			
Unmarked summit ✷	NO		
Lower cairn ✶	NO		

Notes ✷ we didn't
Summit but
Walked the NW
flanks at 600M
above sea-level

Times and Weather			
Departure time			
Arrival time			
Duration			
Weather	WINDY SUNNY		
Visibility	GOOD		

Catstye Cam   890m   2920'   NGR NY348158
Landranger 90   Outdoor Leisure 5

Route from/via	7-9-07			Ascent	Km	Time
Glenridding via 1	DESCENT			730	5.5	
Glenridding via 2				730	5.5c	
Glenridding via 3				730	6.0c	

Ridge routes				Descent	Ascent	Km
Birkhouse Moor				23	195	2.25
Helvellyn 1.105	FROM			125	65	1.0
Helvellyn Lower Man				100	65	1.5

Features visited			
Summit stones	YES		
Swirral Edge	YES		
Red Tarn	NO		

Notes

Times and Weather			
Departure time	4:10		
Arrival time	4:35		
Duration	25MINS		
Weather	V.GOOD		
Visibility	V.GOOD		

Route details: 1 = via Glen-
ridding Beck, 2 = via Mires
Beck, 3 = via Red Tarn Beck.

Clough Head 726m 2382' NGR NY334225
Landranger 90   Outdoor Leisure 5

Route from				Ascent	Km	Time
Dockray				436	7	
Wanthwaite #				556	2.5	
Wanthwaite *				556	4.25	

Ridge routes				Descent	Ascent	Km
Great Dodd				242	111	3.0

Features visited			
Summit cairn			
O.S. trig. point			
Calfhow Pike			

Times and Weather			
Departure time			
Arrival time			
Duration			
Weather			
Visibility			

Notes_____

Route details: # = via Fishers
Wife's Rake, * = via Old Coach
Road.

Dollywaggon Pike 858m 2815' NGR NY346131
Landranger 90   Outdoor Leisure 5 & 7

Route from	6-5-05			Ascent	Km	Time
Dunmail Raise				618	2.75	
Grasmere				788	6.5 - 8.0	
Glenridding				698	6.0 - 7.5	
Patterdale (396159)				708	6.3 - 7.75	
Wythburn (324135)				677	3.25	

Ridge routes				Descent	Ascent	Km
Fairfield	*NO*			338	323	3.25
Nethermost Pike	P.112 *ONTO*			21	12	1.5
Seat Sandal	P.115 *FROM*			162	284	1.5

Features visited			
Summit cairns	YES		
Grisedale Tarn	YES		

Times and Weather			
Departure time	11:28		
Arrival time	13:20		
Duration	1:52		
Weather	COLD,WIND SHOWERS		
Visibility	FAIR		

Notes_ * coffee -
break en route

Dove Crag 792m 2599' NGR NY374105
Landranger 90   Outdoor Leisure 5 & 7

Route from	SEP '96	2-5-02		Ascent	Km	Time
Ambleside				602	7.5c	
Caw Bridge c.p. (403134)				634	5.0	
Patterdale (396159)				642	7.75	
BROTHERSWATER/DOVEDALE		ASCENT				

Ridge routes				Descent	Ascent	Km
Hart Crag P.102	ONTO	ONTO		77	47	1.0
High Pike P.108	FROM			nil	136	1.75
Little Hart Crag				42	197	1.5

Features visited			
Summit cairn	YES	NO	
Priest's hole (cave)	NO	NO	

Notes 2-5-02
A VERY difficult ascent - especially steep at 376111

Times and Weather			
Departure time	?		
Arrival time	?		
Duration	?		
Weather	COOL, SUN, WINDY		
Visibility	V.GOOD		

Fairfield 873m 2864' NGR NY359118
Landranger 90   Outdoor Leisure 5 & 7

Route from	SEP'96			Ascent	Km	Time
Grasmere				813	5.5	
Patterdale via Deepdale				723	7.5	

Ridge routes				Descent	Ascent	Km
Dollywaggon Pike				323	338	3.25
Great Rigg P.101	ONTO			31	138	1.25
Hart Crag P.102	FROM			47	98	1.0
St. Sunday Crag				161	193	2.25
Seat Sandal				141	278	1.5

Features visited			
Summit cairn	YES		
Summit shelter	YES		

Notes

Times and Weather			
Departure time			
Arrival time			
Duration			
Weather	COOL, SUN WINDY		
Visibility	V.GOOD		

Glenridding Dodd   442m   1450'   NGR NY380175
Landranger 90   Outdoor Leisure 5

Route from	2-9-07			Ascent	Km	Time
Glenridding (Blaes Crag)	DESCENT			282	1.5	

Ridge routes				Descent	Ascent	Km
Sheffield Pike P.116	FROM			280	47	1.5

Features visited			
Summit cairn	YES		

Notes
See P.116

Times and Weather			
Departure time	17.00		
Arrival time	17.35		
Duration	35 MINS		
Weather	GOOD		
Visibility	GOOD		

Gowbarrow Fell   481m   1578'   NGR NY407218
Landranger 90   Outdoor Leisure 5

Route from				Ascent	Km	Time
Aira Force c. p. (401201)				321	3.75c	
Dockray				191	1.75	
Ulcat Row (405255)				181	2.5	

Features visited			
O.S. trig. point			

Notes

Times and Weather			
Departure time			
Arrival time			
Duration			
Weather			
Visibility			

Great Dodd   857m   2812'   NGR NY342206
Landranger 90   Outdoor Leisure 5

Route from				Ascent	Km	Time
Fornside via Calfhow Pike				687	3.0c	
Dockray via Groove Beck				567	6.0	
Dockray via Deepdale				567	6.0	
Dockray via High Brow				567	6.5	

Ridge routes				Descent	Ascent	Km
Clough Head				111	242	3.0
Watson's Dodd				14	84	1.5

Features visited				Notes_____
Summit cairn/shelter				_____
Castle Rock (339m)				_____
Randerside (subsidiary top)				_____
				_____

Times and Weather				_____
Departure time				_____
Arrival time				_____
Duration				_____
Weather				_____
Visibility				_____

Great Mell Fell   537m   1762'   NGR NY397254
Landranger 90   Outdoor Leisure 5

Route from				Ascent	Km	Time
Brownrigg Farm (407254)				277	1.5	
A5091 @ 390266				269	1.5	

Features visited				Notes_____
Summit				_____
Summit tumulus				_____
				_____

Times and Weather				_____
Departure time				_____
Arrival time				_____
Duration				_____
Weather				_____
Visibility				_____

Great Rigg   766m   2513'   NGR NY356104
Landranger 90   Outdoor Leisure 5

Route from/via	SEP '96			Ascent	Km	Time
Grasmere via Stone Arthur				706	3.75	
Grasmere/Greenhead Gill				706	3.75	

Ridge routes				Descent	Ascent	Km
Fairfield P. 98	FROM			138	31	1.25
Heron Pike P. 107	ONTO			17	171	2.25

Features visited				Notes_____
Summit cairn	YES			_____
Stone Arthur (476m)				_____
				_____

Times and Weather				_____
Departure time				_____
Arrival time				_____
Duration				_____
Weather	SUN. COOL WINDY			_____
Visibility	V.GOOD			_____

Green Side   795m   2608'   NGR NY353188
Landranger 90   Outdoor Leisure 5

Route from	13-9-07			Ascent	Km	Time
Glencoyne c.p. (386189)	DESCENT			645	4.0c	
Dockray				505	6.0-6.5c	

Ridge routes				Descent	Ascent	Km
Hart Side				21	60	1.25
Raise				138	50	2.25
Stybarrow Dodd (P.116)	FROM			78	30	1.0

Features visited				Notes_____
Summit cairn	YES			_____
				_____

Times and Weather				_____
Departure time				_____
Arrival time				_____
Duration				_____
Weather	DULL			_____
Visibility	GOOD			_____

Hart Crag   822m   2697'   NGR NY368113
Landranger 90   Outdoor Leisure 5 & 7

Route from	SEP '96	2-5-02		Ascent	Km	Time
Caw Bridge c. p. (403134)				664	5.25	
Rydal				762	5.5c	

Ridge routes				Descent	Ascent	Km
Dove Crag P. 98	FROM	FROM		47	77	1.0
Fairfield P. 98	ONTO			98	47	1.0
Hartsop above How P. 103		ONTO		5	257	1.75

Features visited				Notes_____
Summit cairn	YES	YES		

Times and Weather			
Departure time	?	?	
Arrival time	?	?	
Duration	?	?	
Weather	COOL, SUN WINDY	SUNNY	
Visibility	V. GOOD	V. GOOD	

Hart Side   756m   2480'   NGR NY359197
Landranger 90   Outdoor Leisure 5

Route from				Ascent	Km	Time
Dockray				466	5.0	
Glencoyne c. p. (386189)				606	4.0c	

Ridge routes				Descent	Ascent	Km
Green Side				60	21	1.25

Features visited				Notes_____
Summit cairns				

Times and Weather			
Departure time			
Arrival time			
Duration			
Weather			
Visibility			

Hartsop above How   570m   1887'   NGR NY385121
Landranger 90   Outdoor Leisure 5

Route from	2-5-02			Ascent	Km	Time
Caw Bridge c. p. (403134)	DESCENT			412	3.5	
Deepdale Bridge (399144)				420	4.75	

Ridge routes				Descent	Ascent	Km
Hart Crag P. 102	FROM			257	5	1.75

Features visited			
Summit cairns	YES		

Times and Weather			
Departure time			
Arrival time			
Duration			
Weather	SUNNY		
Visibility	V. GOOD		

Notes_____
_____
_____
_____
_____
_____
_____
_____
_____
_____
_____
_____
_____
_____

Helvellyn (1)   950m   3117'   NGR NY342151
Landranger 90   Outdoor Leisure 5

Eastern approaches				Ascent	Km	Time
Thirlspot via Brown Crag #				760	4.75	
Thirlspot via Brown How #				760	4.0	
Thirlmere c. p. (316170) #				730	3.25	
Wythburn (324135) via:						
Comb Gill				769	3.25	
main path				769	3.75	
mine route (324147)				769	3.25	
Whelpside Gill				769	2.75	

Features visited			
Summit cairn			
O.S. trig. point			
Summit rock shelter			
Aeroplane landing tablet			
Gough Memorial			
Dixon Memorial			
Red Tarn			

Times and Weather			
Departure time			
Arrival time			
Duration			
Weather			
Visibility			

Notes_____

_____
_____
_____
_____
_____
_____
_____
_____
_____
_____
_____
_____

Route details: # = via Helvellyn Lower Man.

Helvellyn (2)

Western approaches	10-9-97	7-9-07		Ascent	Km	Time
Glenridding via:						
Striding Edge				790	5.25	
Swirral Edge				790	5.5	
Patterdale via:						
Striding Edge	ASCENT			800	6.0	
Swirral Edge				800	6.0	

Ridge routes(from)/via				Descent	Ascent	Km
Birkhouse Moor via 1	P.95		FROM	23	255	3.0
Birkhouse Moor via 2	P.95	ONTO		23	255	2.7c
Catstye Cam	P.96		ONTO	65	125	1.0
Helvellyn Lower Man				20	45	.5
Nethermost Pike				31	90	1.0

Features visited			
Summit cairn	NO	YES	
O.S. trig. point	YES	YES	
Summit rock shelter	YES	YES	
Aeroplane landing tablet	NO	NO	
Gough Memorial	NO	YES	
Dixon Memorial	NO	YES	
Red Tarn	YES	NO	

Times and Weather			
Departure time	?		
Arrival time	?		
Duration	?		
Weather	HOT SUNNY	V.GOOD	
Visibility	V. GOOD	V.GOOD	

Notes_____
_____
_____
_____
_____
_____
_____
_____
_____
_____
_____
_____
_____

Route details: 1 = via Striding Edge, 2 = via Swirral Edge.

Helvellyn Lower Man   925m   3035'   NGR NY337155
Landranger 90   Outdoor Leisure 5

Route from/via				Ascent	Km	Time
Glenridding/Swirral Edge				765	5.75	
Patterdale via Swirral Edge				775	6.5	
Thirlmere c.p.(316170) via:						
main route				705	3.0	
mine route (324147)				705	4.0	
Thirlspot via:						
Brown Crag				735	4.25	
Brown How				735	3.5	

Ridge routes				Descent	Ascent	Km
Catstye Cam				65	100	1.5
Helvellyn				45	20	.5
Whiteside				68	130	1.25

Features visited			
Summit cairn			

Times and Weather			
Departure time			
Arrival time			
Duration			
Weather			
Visibility			

Notes_____
_____
_____
_____
_____
_____
_____
_____
_____
_____
_____
_____
_____
_____

Heron Pike   612m   2008'   NGR NY356083
Landranger 90   Outdoor Leisure 7

Route from	SEP '96			Ascent	Km	Time
Grasmere				552	2.5	
Rydal				553	2.5	
White Moss Common c. p.				502	2.5	

Ridge routes				Descent	Ascent	Km
Great Rigg	P. 101	FROM		171	17	2.25
Nab Scar	P. 111	ONTO		nil	167	1.25

Features visited			
Summit cairn	YES		
North top (621m) (357087)			

Times and Weather			
Departure time	?		
Arrival time	?		
Duration	?		
Weather	COOL SUNNY		
Visibility	V. GOOD		

Notes_____

High Hartsop Dodd   519m   1703'   NGR NY393107
Landranger 90   Outdoor Leisure 5

Route from				Ascent	Km	Time
Caw Bridge c. p. (403134)				361	3.0	
Hartsop Hall				349	1.5	

Ridge routes				Descent	Ascent	Km
Little Hart Crag				118	nil	1.0

Features visited			
Summit			

Times and Weather			
Departure time			
Arrival time			
Duration			
Weather			
Visibility			

Notes_____

High Pike   656m   2152'   NGR NY373088
Landranger 90   Outdoor Leisure 7

Route from	SEP '96			Ascent	Km	Time
Ambleside via Scandale				566	4.75	

Ridge routes				Descent	Ascent	Km
Dove Crag P. 98	ONTO			136	nil	1.75
Little Hart Crag #				104	123	2.5
Low Pike P. 110	FROM			nil	148	1.0

Features visited			
Summit cairn	YES		

Times and Weather			
Departure time	?		
Arrival time	?		
Duration	?		
Weather	COOL, SUN WINDY		
Visibility	V. GOOD		

Notes_____
_____
_____
_____
_____
_____
_____
_____
_____
_____
_____
_____

Route details: # = the ridge between summits is higher than the summits themselves.

Little Hart Crag   637m   2090'   NGR NY387100
Landranger 90   Outdoor Leisure 5 & 7

Route from				Ascent	Km	Time
Ambleside via Scandale				547	5.75	
Caw Bridge c.p. (403134) via:						
Caiston Glen				479	5.0	
Hoggett Gill				479	5.0	
Patterdale via:						
Caiston Glen				487	7.75	
Hoggett Gill				487	7.75	

Ridge routes				Descent	Ascent	Km
Dove Crag				197	42	1.5
High Hartsop Dodd				nil	118	1.0
High Pike #				123	104	2.5
Middle Dodd				134	117	2.0
Red Screes				256	117	1.75

Features visited			
Summit cairn			
Lower cairn			

Times and Weather			
Departure time			
Arrival time			
Duration			
Weather			
Visibility			

Notes_____

_____
_____
_____
_____
_____
_____
_____
_____
_____
_____
_____
_____

Route details: # = the ridge between summits is higher than the summits themselves

Little Mell Fell   505m   1657'   NGR NY423240
Landranger 90   Outdoor Leisure 5

Route from				Ascent	Km	Time
The Hause (424235)				125	.5	
Lowthwaite				205	2.0c	
Nabend (415250)				205	2.0c	
Thackthwaite				205	1.25	

Features visited			
Summit cairn			
O.S. trig. point			

Times and Weather			
Departure time			
Arrival time			
Duration			
Weather			
Visibility			

Notes_____
_____
_____
_____
_____
_____
_____
_____
_____
_____

Low Pike   508m   1667'   NGR NY373078
Landranger 90   Outdoor Leisure 7

Route from	SEP '96			Ascent	Km	Time
Ambleside via:						
High Sweden Bridge				418	4.0	
Low Sweden Bridge	ASCENT			418	3.5	
Rydal Beck				418	5.0	
Rydal via Rydal Beck				449	3.0	

Ridge routes				Descent	Ascent	Km
High Pike P. 108	ONTO			148	nil	1.0

Features visited			
Summit cairn	YES		
Buckstones Jump			

Times and Weather			
Departure time	?		
Arrival time	?		
Duration	?		
Weather	COOL SUN		
Visibility	V. GOOD		

Notes_____
_____
_____
_____
_____
_____
_____
_____
_____
_____
_____

Middle Dodd   654m   2146'   NGR NY397094
Landranger 90   Outdoor Leisure 5 & 7

Route from	3.9.07			Ascent	Km	Time
Caw Bridge c. p. (403134)				496	4.0	
Hartsop Hall				484	2.5	
Patterdale				504	7.75	

Ridge routes				Descent	Ascent	Km
Little Hart Crag				117	134	2.0
Red Screes P. 114	FROM/TO			131	9	1.0

Features visited			
Summit cairn	YES		

Times and Weather			
Departure time			
Arrival time			
Duration			
Weather	GOOD		
Visibility	V-GOOD		

* Notes 3.9.07 - Did Middle Dodd as an out-and-back detour from Red Screes.

Nab Scar   445m   1460'   NGR NY356072
Landranger 90   Outdoor Leisure 7

Route from	SEP '96			Ascent	Km	Time
Rydal	DESCENT			386	1.5	
White Moss Common c. p.				403	1.25	

Ridge routes				Descent	Ascent	Km
Heron Pike	FROM			167	nil	1.25

Features visited			
Summit cairn	YES		

Times and Weather			
Departure time	?		
Arrival time	?		
Duration	?		
Weather	HOT/SUNNY		
Visibility	V-GOOD		

Notes _____

Nethermost Pike   891m   2923'   NGR NY344142
Landranger 90   Outdoor Leisure 5

Route from/via	6-5-05			Ascent	Km	Time
Patterdale via East ridge				741	6.75	
Dunmail Raise/Birkside Gill	DESCENT			651	3.0	11:50
Wythburn (342135) via:						
Birkside Gill				710	4.25	
Comb Gill				710	2.5	
main path				710	3.0	
Whelpside Gill				710	2.5	

Ridge routes				Descent	Ascent	Km
Dollywaggon Pike	FROM			12	21	1.5
Helvellyn	NO			90	31	1.0

Features visited			
Summit cairn	YES		
Hard Tarn	NO		

Times and Weather			
Departure time	13:20		
Arrival time	14:00		
Duration	✳ 6:40		
Weather	V. COLD V. WINDY		
Visibility	FAIR		

Notes ✳ Quick lunch break en route. The very
cold wind deterred us from stopping for long

Raise   883m   2897'   NGR NY343174
Landranger 90   Outdoor Leisure 5

Route from	14-9-07			Ascent	Km	Time
Glencoyne c. p./Sticks Gill				733	5.75c	
Glenridding/Stang End				723	5.0	
Glenridding/Keppel Cove				723	5.5	
Stanah				683	3.25	
Thirlspot via Brund Gill				693	3.25	
Thirlspot via Sticks Gill				693	3.5	

Ridge routes				Descent	Ascent	Km
Green Side				50	138	2.25
Sheffield Pike				85	293	3.0c
Stybarrow Dodd	P.116	ONTO		98	138	1.75
White Side		FROM		38	58	1.0

Features visited		
Summit cairn	YES	
Derelict chimney	NO	

Times and Weather		
Departure time		
Arrival time		
Duration		
Weather	DULL, COLD	
Visibility	GOOD	

Notes_____
_____
_____
_____
_____
_____
_____
_____
_____
_____
_____
_____
_____

Red Screes   776m   2456'   NGR NY396088
Landranger 90   Outdoor Leisure 5 & 7

MIDDLE
GROVE

Route from/via	39.07			Ascent	Km	Time
Ambleside/~~Scandale Pass~~	ASCENT			686	6.5	
Caw Bridge c. p. (403134)				618	5.5	
Hartsop Hall				606	4.0	
Kirkstone Pass Inn				331	1.0	
AMBLESIDE	DESCENT					

Ridge routes				Descent	Ascent	Km
Little Hart Crag				117	256	1.75
Middle Dodd P.111	ONTO			9	131	1.0

Features visited			
Summit cairn	YES		
O.S. trig. point	YES		
Summit tarns	YES		
The Kirk Stone	NO		

Times and Weather			
Departure time	10:15		
Arrival time	13:00		
Duration	2' 45"		
Weather	GOOD		
Visibility	V GOOD		

Notes_____

Saint Sunday Crag   841m   2759'   NGR NY369134
Landranger 90   Outdoor Leisure 5

Route from/via	2.5-05			Ascent	Km	Time
Dunmail Raise/Grisedale Tarn				601	4.75	
Patterdale	DESCENT			791	4.0	

Ridge routes				Descent	Ascent	Km
Arnison Crag	NO			18	426	3.25
Birks	FROM			19	238	1.5
Fairfield	NO			193	161	2.25

Features visited			
Summit cairn	YES		
Gavel Pike	NO		
Lord's Seat	NO		

Notes ✱ Slow going after running the Keswick 1/2 Marathon on 1st May, and bird-watching stops.

Times and Weather			
Departure time	10:43		
Arrival time	13:23		
Duration ✱	2' 40"		
Weather	WINDY SUNNY		
Visibility	GOOD		

Seat Sandal   736m   2415'   NGR NY344115
Landranger 90   Outdoor Leisure 5

Route from/via	6-5-05			Ascent	Km	Time
Dunmail Raise	ASCENT			496	2.25	1' 20"
Grasmere via Tongue Gill				676	5.0	
Grasmere/Little Tongue Gill				676	5.25	
Patterdale				586	7.75	

Ridge routes				Descent	Ascent	Km
Fairfield	P.98	NO		278	141	1.5
Dollywaggon Pike	P.97	ONTO		284	162	1.5

Features visited			
Summit cairn	YES		

Notes _____

Times and Weather			
Departure time	10:08		
Arrival time	11:28		
Duration	1:20		
Weather	COLD, WINDY SHOWERS		
Visibility	FAIR		

Sheffield Pike   675m   2215'   NGR NY369182
Landranger 90   Outdoor Leisure 5

Route from	2-9-07			Ascent	Km	Time
Glencoyne c. p. # _Heron Pike_	ASCENT			525	3.5	
Glenridding via lead mine				515	4.0	

Ridge routes				Descent	Ascent	Km
Glenridding Dodd P.99	ONTO			47	280	1.5
Raise				293	85	3.0c
Stybarrow Dodd				263	95	3.5

Features visited			
Summit cairn	YES		
Black Crag	NO		
Heron Pike	YES		

Times and Weather			
Departure time GILLSIDE	14:00		
Arrival time	16:50		
Duration	2:50		
Weather	GOOD		
Visibility	GOOD		

Notes 2-9-07
Perfect walking
weather but cold
westerly wind on
summit

Route details: # = via Seldom
Seen.

Stybarrow Dodd   843m   2766'   NGR NY343189
Landranger 90   Outdoor Leisure 5

Route from	14-9-07			Ascent	Km	Time
Stanah via Stanah Gill				643	2.25	
Sticks Pass				643	3.25	
Dockray via Deepdale				553	6.75	

Ridge routes				Descent	Ascent	Km
Green Side (P.101)	ONTO			30	78	1.0
Raise (P.113)	FROM			138	98	1.75
Sheffield Pike				95	263	3.5
Watson's Dodd				14	68	1.0

Features visited			
Summit cairn	YES		

Times and Weather			
Departure time			
Arrival time			
Duration			
Weather	DULL COLD		
Visibility	GOOD		

Notes Boring summit
but great Panorama

Watson's Dodd   789m   2589' NGR NY336196
Landranger 90   Outdoor Leisure 5

Route from/via			Ascent	Km	Time
Legburthwaite (318195)			659	2.25	
Legburthwaite/Castle Rock			659	2.5	

Ridge routes			Descent	Ascent	Km
Great Dodd			82	14	1.5
Stybarrow Dodd			68	14	1.0

Features visited				Notes_____
Summit cairn				
Castle Rock				

Times and Weather			
Departure time			
Arrival time			
Duration			
Weather			
Visibility			

White Side   863m   2832' NGR NY338167
Landranger 90   Outdoor Leisure 5

Route from	149.07		Ascent	Km	Time
Glenridding	ASCENT		703	5.5	
Stanah			663	3.0	
Thirlspot			733	3.75	

Ridge routes			Descent	Ascent	Km
Helvellyn Lower Man			130	68	1.25
Raise P. 113	ONTO		58	38	1.0

Features visited				Notes_____
Summit cairn	YES			

Times and Weather			
Departure time			
Arrival time			
Duration			
Weather	DULL COLD		
Visibility	GOOD		

CHAPTER SEVEN

FAR EASTERN LAKE DISTRICT

Mountain	Page	Height in Metres	Date first Ascended
Angletarn Pikes	119	567	2.9.99 (21)
Arthur's Pike	120	532	__:__:__
Beda Fell	120	509	__:__:__
Bonscale Pike	121	530	__:__:__
Branstree	121	713	__:__:__
Brock Crags	122	561	__:__:__
Froswick	122	720	__:__:__
Gray Crag	123	699	__:__:__
Grey Crag	123	638	__:__:__
Hallin Fell	124	388	__:__:__
Harrop Pike	124	637	__:__:__
Harter Fell	125	778	__:__:__
Hartsop Dodd	126	618	__:__:__
High Raise	126	802	__:__:__
High Street	127	828	30.8.97
Ill Bell	128	757	__:__:__
Kentmere Pike	128	730	__:__:__
Kidsty Pike	129	780	__:__:__
The Knott	129	739	6.5.02
Loadpot Hill	130	671	__:__:__
Mardale Ill Bell	131	760	30.8.97
The Nab	132	576	__:__:__
Place Fell	132	657	5.9.99
Rampsgill Head	133	792	6.5.02
Rest Dodd	134	696	__:__:__
Rough Crag	135	628	30.8.97
Sallows	135	516	__:__:__
Selside Pike	136	655	__:__:__
Shipman Knotts	136	587	__:__:__
Sour Howes	137	483	__:__:__
Steel Knotts	137	432	__:__:__
Stoney Cove Pike	138	763	6.5.02
Tarn Crag	138	664	__:__:__
Thornthwaite Crag	139	784	6.5.02
Troutbeck Tongue	139	364	__:__:__
Wansfell & Wansfell Pike	140	487/476	6.9.97
Wether Hill	140	670	__:__:__
Yoke	141	706	__:__:__

Angletarn Pikes   567m   1860'   NGR NY413148
Landranger 90   Outdoor Leisure 5

Route from	29-99	6-9-07	Ascent	Km	Time
Dale Head (433165) via 1			357	3.75	
Dale Head via 2		ASCENT	357	3.5	
Dale Head via 3			357	2.75	
Hartsop via 1			397	4.0	
Patterdale (396159) via 1	ASCENT	DESCENT	417	2.75	
11 via Hartsop	DESCENT				

Ridge routes			Descent	Ascent	Km
Beda Fell			64	122	3.0
Brock Crags			81	87	2.25
The Knott			259	87	3.5
Place Fell			287	197	2.5
Rest Dodd			216	87	2.75

Features visited			
Summit cairn (567m)	NO	NO	
South summit (565m)	NO	YES	
Angle Tarn	YES	YES	

Times and Weather			
Departure time	?		
Arrival time	?		
Duration	?		
Weather	MISTY	V. GOOD	
Visibility	ZERO	V. GOOD	

Notes Strictly speaking, we did it do these Pikes in 1999 due to poor visibility. We only walked along the base of them. Finally summitted in 2007.

Route details: 1 = via Boredale Hause, 2 = via Bannerdale & Angle Tarn, 3 = via Heckbeck Head.

Arthur's Pike   532m   1745'   NGR NY461206
Landranger 90   Outdoor Leisure 5

Route from				Ascent	Km	Time
Askham				330	6.25	
Helton				322	6.25	
Howtown via #				382	6.0c	
Howtown via *				382	3.0c	
Pooley Bridge				382	5.5	

Ridge routes				Descent	Ascent	Km
Bonscale Pike				30	32	1.25
Loadpot Hill				139	nil	3.0

Features visited				Notes_____
Summit cairn				
White Knott Reservoir				

Times and Weather			
Departure time			
Arrival time			
Duration			
Weather			
Visibility			

Route details: # = via Barton
Fell, * = via Swarthbeck Gill.

Beda Fell   509m   1670'   NGR NY428171
Landranger 90   Outdoor Leisure 5

Route from				Ascent	Km	Time
Boredale Head (419171)				319	4.25	
Martindale via Nickies				296	2.5	
Martindale via Winter Crag				296	2.75	
Sandwick via Winter Crag				359	2.75	

Ridge routes				Descent	Ascent	Km
Angletarn Pikes				122	64	3.0
Place Fell				267	119	4.0

Features visited				Notes_____
Summit cairn				

Times and Weather			
Departure time			
Arrival time			
Duration			
Weather			
Visibility			

Bonscale Pike   530m   1739'   NGR NY454201
Landranger 90   Outdoor Leisure 5

Route from				Ascent	Km	Time
Howtown via:						
Swarthbeck Gill				380	3.0	
Mellguards/Swarth Fell path				380	2.5	

Ridge routes				Descent	Ascent	Km
Arthur's Pike				32	30	1.25
Loadpot Hill				141	nil	2.5

Features visited				Notes_____
Summit cairn				
Bonscale Tower				
Higher (smaller) pillar				

Times and Weather				
Departure time				
Arrival time				
Duration				
Weather				
Visibility				

Branstree   713m   2345'   NGR NY478100
Landranger 90   Outdoor Leisure 5 & 7

Route from				Ascent	Km	Time
Mardale Head				461	2.5	
Sadgill (483057)				518	4.5	

Ridge routes				Descent	Ascent	Km
Harrop Pike				211 *	287 *	3.75
Harter Fell				203	138	2.5
Selside Pike				13	71	1.75
Tarn Crag				169	218	2.5

Features visited				Notes _____
O.S.trig. point				
North East top (673m)				
Artlecrag Pike Beacon				
Survey Pillar				

Times and Weather				
Departure time				
Arrival time				
Duration				
Weather				
Visibility				

Route details: * = approximate using the route via Tarn Crag (NY488078).

Brock Crags   561m   1841'   NGR NY417136
Landranger 90   Outdoor Leisure 5

Route from				Ascent	Km	Time
Hartsop via:						
Angle Tarn				391	3.25c	
top of Calfgate Hill				391	2.5c	

Ridge routes				Descent	Ascent	Km
Angletarn Pikes				87	81	2.25
The Knott				214	36	2.5
Rest Dodd				178	43	1.5

Features visited			
Summit cairn			

Notes _____

Times and Weather			
Departure time			
Arrival time			
Duration			
Weather			
Visibility			

Froswick   720m   2362'   NGR NY435085
Landranger 90   Outdoor Leisure 7

Route from/via				Ascent	Km	Time
Troutbeck via Blue Gill				540	6.26	
Troutbeck/Park Fell path				540	7.75	

Ridge routes				Descent	Ascent	Km
High Street				198	90	3.0
Ill Bell				62	25	.75
Thornthwaite Crag				64	nil	1.5

Features visited			
Summit cairn			

Notes _____

Times and Weather			
Departure time			
Arrival time			
Duration			
Weather			
Visibility			

Gray Crag   699m   2293'   NGR NY428117
Landranger 90   Outdoor Leisure 5 & 72

Route from				Ascent	Km	Time
Hartsop direct				529	2.75	
Hartsop #				529	5.0	

Ridge routes				Descent	Ascent	Km
Thornthwaite Crag				85	small	1.75

Features visited			
Summit			

Times and Weather			
Departure time			
Arrival time			
Duration			
Weather			
Visibility			

Notes _____

_____

_____

_____

_____

_____

_____

Route details: # = via Threshthwaite Mouth.

Grey Crag   638m   2093'   NGR NY497072
Landranger 90   Outdoor Leisure 7

Route from				Ascent	Km	Time
Sadgill (483057) & Gt. Howe				443	2.25	
*						

Ridge routes				Descent	Ascent	Km
Harrop Pike				12	13	.75
Tarn Crag				69	43	2.0

Features visited			
Summit cairn			
Great Howe survey post			

Times and Weather			
Departure time			
Arrival time			
Duration			
Weather			
Visibility			

Notes _____

_____

_____

_____

_____

Route details: * = several long
approaches from the A6 are
possible over ridges through
valleys and a combination of
both. Rights of way and
paths do not exist, but space
is left should you wish to try.

Hallin Fell   388m   1273'   NGR NY433198
Landranger 90   Outdoor Leisure 5

Route from	*6-9-07*			Ascent	Km	Time
Howtown	*ASCENT + DESCENT*			238	1.5	
Martindale old church #				158	.75	

Features visited				Notes _____
Summit obelisk	*YES*			

Times and Weather			
Departure time			
Arrival time			
Duration			
Weather	*V.GOOD*		
Visibility	*V.GOOD*		

Route details: # = from Saint
Peter's Church.

Harrop Pike   637m   2090'   NGR NY501078
Landranger 90   Outdoor Leisure 7

Route from				Ascent	Km	Time
Sadgill via #				442+	3.0c	
*						

Ridge routes				Descent	Ascent	Km
Branstree				287+	211+	3.75
Grey Crag				13	12	.75
Tarn Crag				69	42	1.75c

Features visited				Notes_____
Summit cairn				
Summit windshelter				
Tarn				

Route details: # = via Great
Crag and Great Howe,

Times and Weather			
Departure time			
Arrival time			
Duration			
Weather			
Visibility			

* = several long approaches
from the A6 are possible over
ridges through valleys and a
combination of both. Rights
of way and paths do not exist,
but space is left should you
wish to try.

Harter Fell   778m   2553'   NGR NY460093
Landranger 90   Outdoor Leisure 5 & 7

Route from/via				Ascent	Km	Time
Kentmere/Nan Bield Pass				608	7.0	
Mardale Head/G'garth Pass				526	3.25	
Mardale Head/N.Bield Pass				526	3.0	
Sadgill via Gatesgarth Pass				583	5.5	
Sadgill via Wrengill				583	5.5	

Ridge routes				Descent	Ascent	Km
Branstree				138	203	2.5
Kentmere Pike				35	83	1.75
Mardale Ill Bell				250	268	1.5

Features visited			
Summit cairn			
Nan Bield			
Adam Seat (666m)			
Small Water			
Small Water stone shelters			

Times and Weather			
Departure time			
Arrival time			
Duration			
Weather			
Visibility			

Notes _____

_____
_____
_____
_____
_____
_____
_____
_____
_____
_____
_____
_____
_____
_____

Hartsop Dodd   618m   2028' NGR NY411119
Landranger 90   Outdoor Leisure 5

Route from				Ascent	Km	Time
Brotherswater Inn				438	1.25	
Cauldale Bridge				427	1.25	
Hartsop via North Ridge				448	1.5	

Ridge routes				Descent	Ascent	Km
Stoney Cove Pike				168	23	2.0

Features visited			
Summit wall/cairn			
Large cairn			

Times and Weather			
Departure time			
Arrival time			
Duration			
Weather			
Visibility			

Notes _____

High Raise   802m   2631' NGR NY448135
Landranger 90   Outdoor Leisure 5

Route from				Ascent	Km	Time
Dale Head (433165) #				592	5.0	
Mardale Head *				550	5.5c	

Ridge routes				Descent	Ascent	Km
Kidsty Pike				30	52	1.0
Rampsgill Head				42	52	1.0
Wether Hill				15	147	3.25

Features visited			
Summit cairn			
Summit windshelter			
Low Raise (754m)			

Times and Weather			
Departure time			
Arrival time			
Duration			
Weather			
Visibility			

Notes _____

Route details: # = via Red
Crag and Mere Beck. This
crosses over the private land
of Martindale Deer Forest for
which permission to use this
access should be sought.
* = via Randale Beck.

High Street 828m 2717' NGR NY441110
Landranger 90 Outdoor Leisure 5 & 7

Route from	30-8-97 65-02			Ascent	Km	Time
Kentmere via Hall Cove				658	8.0	
Mardale Head #				576	3.25	
Mardale Head *				576	5.25	
Troutbeck via Scott Rake				648	8.5	

Ridge routes				Descent	Ascent	Km
Froswick				90	198	3.0
Kidsty Pike				65	113	2.5
The Knott	P. 129	—	ONTO *	24	113	1.75
Mardale Ill Bell	P.131	ONTO	—	15	83	1.25
Rough Crag	P.135	FROM	—	nil	200	1.5
Thornthwaite Crag	P.139	—	FROM	34	78	1.5

Features visited			
Summit cairn	YES	NO	
O.S. trig. point	YES	NO	
Roman Road	YES	YES	
Summit Wall	YES	NO	

Times and Weather			
Departure time	?	14:20	
Arrival time	?	14:40	
Duration	?	20 MINS	
Weather	HOT/SUNNY	WINDY MISTY	
Visibility	V. GOOD	POOR	

Notes * via Ramsgill Head, by mistake in the mist!
(See page 139)

Route details: # = via Blea Water and Caspel Gate excluding Rough Crag ridge route, * = via Riggindale Crag including Rough Crag ridge route.

Ill Bell   757m   2484'   NGR NY436077
Landranger 90   Outdoor Leisure 7

Route from				Ascent	Km	Time
Kentmere #				587	6.25	
Troutbeck via Quarry path				577	6.0	

Ridge routes				Descent	Ascent	Km
Froswick				25	62	.75
Yoke				41	92	1.0

Features visited				Notes_____
Summit cairns *				_____
				_____

Times and Weather			
Departure time			
Arrival time			
Duration			
Weather			
Visibility			

Route details: # = via Leads Howe Ridge, * = One of the cairns was vandalised in August 1994.

Kentmere Pike   730m   2395'   NGR NY466078
Landranger 90   Outdoor Leisure 7

Route from/via				Ascent	Km	Time
Brockstones (466062)				480	2.75	
Kentmere				560	4.25	
Sadgill (483057)/Steel Rigg				535	4.25	

Ridge routes				Descent	Ascent	Km
Harter Fell				83	35	1.75
Shipman Knotts				7	150	1.75

Features visited				Notes_____
Summit cairn				_____
O.S. trig. point				_____
Goat Scar (cairned)				_____
				_____

Times and Weather			
Departure time			
Arrival time			
Duration			
Weather			
Visibility			

Kidsty Pike   780m   2559'   NGR NY447126
Landranger 90   Outdoor Leisure 5

Route from				Ascent	Km	Time
Mardale via Kidsty Howes				528	4.0	

Ridge routes				Descent	Ascent	Km
High Raise				52	30	1.0
High Street				113	65	2.5
Rampsgill Head				27	15	.5

Features visited			
Summit cairn			

Notes _____

Times and Weather			
Departure time			
Arrival time			
Duration			
Weather			
Visibility			

The Knott   739m   2425'   NGR NY437127
Landranger 90   Outdoor Leisure 5

Route from/via	6-5.02			Ascent	Km	Time
Hartsop via filter house				569	3.25	
Hartsop/Calfgate Gill Head				569	4.0	
HARTSOP / CAUDALE BRIDGE	DESCENT			548	5.0	1H 30M

Ridge routes				Descent	Ascent	Km
Angletarn Pikes				87	259	3.5
Brock Crags				36	214	2.5
High Street				113	24	1.75
Rampsgill Head P.133	FROM			66	13	.75
Rest Dodd				111	154	1.0
Rough Crag				105	216	3.0

Features visited			
Summit	YES		

Notes _____

Times and Weather			
Departure time	15:30		
Arrival time	15:45		
Duration	15 MINS		
Weather	MISTY		
Visibility	POOR		

Loadpot Hill   671m   2202'   NGR NY456182
Landranger 90   Outdoor Leisure 5

Route from			Ascent	Km	Time
Bampton			491	6.0c	
Helton			461	7.5c	
Howtown via Dodd Gill			521	3.0	
Martindale via Groove Gill			458	4.5	
Pooley Bridge			521	8.5c	

Ridge routes			Descent	Ascent	Km
Arthur's Pike			nil	139	3.0
Bonscale Pike			nil	141	2.5
Steel Knotts			232	451	3.25
Wether Hill			48	49	1.5

Features visited			
Summit cairn			
O.S. trig. point			
Lowther House ruins			

Times and Weather			
Departure time			
Arrival time			
Duration			
Weather			
Visibility			

Notes_____

_____

_____

_____

_____

_____

_____

_____

_____

_____

_____

_____

_____

Mardale III Bell   760m   2495'   NGR NY448101
Landranger 90   Outdoor Leisure 5 & 7

Route from	30-8-97			Ascent	Km	Time
Kentmere/Lingmell End				590	7.5	
Kentmere/Nan Bield Pass				590	7.0	
Mardale Head #	DESCENT			508	3.0	?
Mardale Head/Piot Crag				508	2.5	

Ridge routes				Descent	Ascent	Km
Harter Fell				268	250	1.5
High Street P.127	FROM			83	15	1.25
Thornthwaite Crag				29	2	5.0

Features visited			
Summit cairn	YES		
Lingmell end (660m)			
Nan Bield	YES		
Blea Water			
Small Water	YES		
Small Water stone shelters	YES		

Times and Weather			
Departure time	?		
Arrival time	?		
Duration	?		
Weather	HOT SUNNY		
Visibility	V. GOOD		

Notes_____

Route details: # = via Nan Bield Pass.

The Nab   576m   1890'   NGR NY434152
Landranger 90   Outdoor Leisure 5

Route from				Ascent	Km	Time
Dale Head (433165) #				366	2.5	
Dale Head *				366	1.75	

Ridge routes				Descent	Ascent	Km
Rest Dodd				181	61	1.5

Features visited			
Summit cairn			

Times and Weather			
Departure time			
Arrival time			
Duration			
Weather			
Visibility			

Notes_____
_____
_____
_____
_____

Route details: # = via North ridge and path, 2 = via West side path. The Nab lies on private land. permission to walk to the summit should be sought.

Place Fell   657m   2156'   NGR NY406170
Landranger 90   Outdoor Leisure 5

Route from	5.9.99			Ascent	Km	Time
Boredale Head (419171) #				467	3.0	
Martindale old church *				444	4.0	
Patterdale (396159) #	ASCENT			507	3.5	
Patterdale 1				507	3.75	
Sandwick	DESCENT			507	3.5 - 4.0	?

Ridge routes				Descent	Ascent	Km
Angletarn Pikes				197	287	2.5
Beda Fell				119	267	4.0

Features visited			
O.S. trig. point	YES		
The Knight			

Times and Weather			
Departure time	?		
Arrival time	?		
Duration	?		
Weather	HOT SUNNY		
Visibility	V. GOOD		

Notes_____
_____
_____
_____
_____
_____
_____

Route details: # = via Boredale Hause, * = from Saint Peter's Church, 1 = via Hare Shaw (401178).

Rampsgill Head   792m   2599'   NGR NY443128
Landranger 90   Outdoor Leisure 5

Route from	6-5-02			Ascent	Km	Time
Mardale Head #				540	4.75	
Mardale Head *				540	6.5	
Hartsop 1				622	4.0	
Hartsop 2				622	4.75	

Ridge routes				Descent	Ascent	Km
High Raise				52	42	1.0
High Street	P. 127	FROM		113	77	2.0
Kidsty Pike				15	27	.5
The Knott	P. 129	ONTO		13	66	.75
Rough Crag				105	269	3.0

Features visited			
Summit cairns	YES		

Times and Weather			
Departure time	14:40		
Arrival time	15:10		
Duration	30 MINS		
Weather	WINDY MISTY		
Visibility	POOR		

Notes   6-5-02. Had not intended to bag this Summit, but we got disorientated in the mist on the way from High Street to The Knott.

Route details: # = via Caspel Gate and Riggindale Crag, excluding Rough Crag ridge route, * = via The Rigg and Riggindale Crag, including Rough Crag ridge route, 1 = via filter house but ignoring The Knott, 2 = via Prison Head Gill.

Rest Dodd   696m   2284'   NGR NY433137
Landranger 90   Outdoor Leisure 5

Route from/via				Ascent	Km	Time
Dale Head (433165) #				486	4.5	
Dale Head *				486	3.0	
Hartsop				526	3.75	
Patterdale/Boredale Hause				546	5.25	

Ridge routes				Descent	Ascent	Km
Angletarn Pikes				87	216	2.75
Brock Crags				43	178	1.5
The Knott				154	111	1.0
The Nab				61	181	1.5

Features visited			
Summit cairns (3)			

Times and Weather			
Departure time			
Arrival time			
Duration			
Weather			
Visibility			

Notes _____
_____
_____
_____
_____
_____
_____
_____
_____
_____
_____
_____
_____
_____

Route details: # = via Bannerdale path, and Satura Crag. * = via Yewgrove Gill.

Rough Crag   628m   2060'   NGR NY454112
Landranger 90   Outdoor Leisure 5

Route from/via	30-8-97			Ascent	Km	Time
Mardale Head/Caspel Gate				376	2.75	
Mardale Head/The Rigg	ASCENT			376	3.5	

Ridge routes				Descent	Ascent	Km
High Street P. 127	ONTO			200	nil	1.5
The Knott				216	105	3.0
Rampsgill Head				269	105	3.0

Features visited				Notes_____
Summit cairn	YES			
Blea Water				
Small Water	YES			
Small Water stone shelters	YES			

Times and Weather			
Departure time	?		
Arrival time	?		
Duration	?		
Weather	HOT/SUNNY		
Visibility	V. GOOD		

Sallows   516m   1693'   NGR NY436040
Landranger 90   Outdoor Leisure 7

Route from				Ascent	Km	Time
Kentmere via:						
Garburn Pass				346	2.75	
Kentmere Hall				346	2.25	
Whiteside End				346	3.75	
Ings				406	7.0	
Troutbeck				176	4.0	

Ridge routes				Descent	Ascent	Km
Yoke				259	69	2.75

Features visited				Notes_____
Summit				

Times and Weather			
Departure time			
Arrival time			
Duration			
Weather			
Visibility			

Selside Pike   655m   2149'   NGR NY490112
Landranger 90   Outdoor Leisure 5

Route from				Ascent	Km	Time
Haweswater Road (479118)				385	2.75	
Mardale Head #				403	4.0	
Swindale Head (505126) *				350	2.5	
Swindale Head 1				350	3.5	

Ridge routes				Descent	Ascent	Km
Branstree				71	13	1.75

Features visited			
Summit cairn			

Notes_____
_____
_____
_____

Times and Weather			
Departure time			
Arrival time			
Duration			
Weather			
Visibility			

Route details: # = via old corpse road, * = via Selside End, 1 = via Swine Gill and fence.

Shipman Knotts   587m   1926'   NGR NY472063
Landanger 90   Outdoor Leisure 7

Route from/via				Ascent	Km	Time
Brockstones (466062)				337	2.25	
Kentmere/Nunnery Beck				417	3.75	
Kentmere/Hallow Bank				417	4.0	
Sadgill via Wray Crag				392	2.75	

Ridge routes				Descent	Ascent	Km
Kentmere Pike				150	7	1.75
Sour Howes				73	106	1.5

Features visited			
Summit			

Notes_____
_____
_____
_____

Times and Weather			
Departure time			
Arrival time			
Duration			
Weather			
Visibility			

Sour Howes 483m 1585' NGR NY428032
Landranger 90   Outdoor Leisure 7

Route from/via				Ascent	Km	Time
High Borrans (433009)				278	2.75	
Kentmere				313	4.0	
Troutbeck/Garburn Pass				303	5.0	

Ridge routes				Descent	Ascent	Km
Sallows				106	73	1.5

Features visited				Notes
Summit cairn				
Capple Howe (445m)				

Times and Weather			
Departure time			
Arrival time			
Duration			
Weather			
Visibility			

Steel Knotts 432m 1417' NGR NY440181
Landranger 90   Outdoor Leisure 5

Route from				Ascent	Km	Time
Howtown via North ridge				282	1.75	
Howtown via Lanty Tarn				282	2.25	
Martindale old church #				219	1.25	

Ridge routes				Descent	Ascent	Km
Loadpot Hill				451	232	3.25
Wether Hill				245	7	2.75

Features visited				Notes
Summit tor (Pikeawassa)				

Times and Weather			
Departure time			
Arrival time			
Duration			
Weather			
Visibility			

Route details: # = from Saint
Peter's Church.

Stoney Cove Pike   763m   2503'   NGR NY418100
(John Bell's Banner, Cauldale Moor)   Landranger 90   Outdoor Leisure 5 & 7

Route from	6-5-02			Ascent	Km	Time
Cauldale Bridge	ASCENT			572	3.0	
Hartsop #				593	4.75	
Kirkstone Pass Inn				369	2.75	
Troutbeck via Hart Crag				583	8.0	
Troutbeck #				583	8.75	

Ridge routes				Descent	Ascent	Km
Hartsop Dodd				23	168	2.0
Thornthwaite Crag P.139	ONTO			189	168	1.5

Features visited			
Summit cairn	YES		
John Bell's Banner			
Mark Atkinson's Monument			
Hart Crag (Woundale) cairn			

Times and Weather			
Departure time	10:20		
Arrival time	12:10		
Duration			
Weather	SUNNY		
Visibility	V.GOOD		

Notes Very Strong winds 26-5-82

_____

_____

_____

_____

_____

_____

_____

_____

Route details: # = via Threshthwaite Mouth.

Tarn Crag   664m   2179'   NGR NY488078
Landranger 90   Outdoor Leisure 7

Route from				Ascent	Km	Time
Sadgill (483057) #				469	2.75	
Sadgill via quarry road *				469	3.75	

Ridge routes				Descent	Ascent	Km
Branstree				218	169	2.5
Grey Crag				43	69	2.0
Harrop Pike				42	69	1.75c

Features visited			
Summit cairn			
Great Howe survey post			

Times and Weather			
Departure time			
Arrival time			
Duration			
Weather			
Visibility			

Notes_____

_____

_____

_____

_____

_____

Route details: # = via Great Howe, * = via quarry road and West ridge.

Thornthwaite Crag   784m   2572'   NGR NY432100
Landranger 90   Outdoor Leisure 5 & 7

Route from	6-5-02			Ascent	Km	Time
Hartsop via Hayeswater				614	5.0	
Hartsop #				614	4.0	
Kentmere via K'mere Res.				614	7.5	
Troutbeck via Scott Rake				604	7.5	
Troutbeck #				604	8.0	

Ridge routes				Descent	Ascent	Km
Froswick				nil	64	1.5
Gray Crag				small	85	1.75
High Street	P- 127	ONTO		78	34	1.5
Mardale III Bell				5	29	2.0
Stoney Cove Pike	P. 138	FROM		168	189	1.5

Features visited			
Summit Beacon	YES		

Notes Note change in weather from S. Cove Pike - P.138 !

Times and Weather			
Departure time	13:30		
Arrival time	14:10		
Duration	40 min		
Weather	MISTY		
Visibility	POOR		

Route details: # = via Threshthwaite Mouth.

Troutbeck Tongue   364m   1194'   NGR NY422064
Landranger 90   Outdoor Leisure 7

Route from				Ascent	Km	Time
Troutbeck via South flank				184	4.0	
Troutbeck via North flank				184	6.5c	

Features visited			
Summit cairn			
Ancient North cairns			

Notes

Times and Weather			
Departure time			
Arrival time			
Duration			
Weather			
Visibility			

Wansfell Pike   476m   1562'   NGR NY394042
Wansfell   487m   1599'   NGR NY430053 *396043*
Landranger 90   Outdoor Leisure 5 7

Route from	6997			Ascent	Km	Time
Ambleside	ASCENT			386 - 397	1.75	
Troutbeck	DESCENT			296 - 307	2.00	?

Ridge routes				Descent	Ascent	Km
Stoney Cove Pike				399	120-123	5.5 - 6.5

Features visited				Notes
Summit	YES			
O.S. trig. point	YES			
N summit (487m)	YES			
Stock Ghyll Force	YES			

Times and Weather			
Departure time	?		
Arrival time	?		
Duration	?		
Weather	DULL		
Visibility	FAIR		

Wether Hill   670m   2198'   NGR NY456167
Landranger 90   Outdoor Leisure 5

Route from				Ascent	Km	Time
Bampton				490	7.5	
Howtown				520	3.5	
Martindale old church #				457	4.0	

Ridge routes				Descent	Ascent	Km
High Raise				147	15	3.25
Loadpot Hill				49	48	1.5
Steel Knotts				7	245	2.75

Features visited				Notes
Summit				

Times and Weather			
Departure time			
Arrival time			
Duration			
Weather			
Visibility			

Route details: # = from Saint Peter's Church.

Yoke   706m   2316'   NGR NY438067
Landranger 90   Outdoor Leisure 7

Route from				Ascent	Km	Time
Kentmere direct #				536	4.0	
Kentmere via Garburn Pass				536	4.25	

Ridge routes				Descent	Ascent	Km
Ill Bell				92	41	1.0
Sallows				69	259	2.75

Features visited			
Summit cairn			
Boundary Stone			
Castle Crag (490m)			

Times and Weather			
Departure time			
Arrival time			
Duration			
Weather			
Visibility			

Notes

Route details: # = via Castle Crag.

CHAPTER EIGHT

SOUTHERN LAKE DISTRICT

Mountain	Page	Height in Metres	Date first Ascended
Allen Crags	143	785	___:___:___
Black Fell	143	322	
Black Sails	144	745	11:5:05
Bowfell	~~144~~ 145	902	9.9.99
Brim Fell	~~144~~ 146	796	11:5:05
Broad Crag	~~144~~ 147	934	9.9.97
Brown Pike	~~144~~ 147	682	11:5:05
Buck Pike	~~144~~ 148	744	11:5:05
Cold Pike	~~144~~ 148	701	
The Old Man of Coniston	~~144~~ 149	803	11:5:02 + 11-5-0
Crinkle Crags	~~144~~ 150	859	6.9.99
Dow Crag	~~144~~ 151	778	11:5:05
Esk Pike	~~144~~ 152	885	9.9.99
Glaramara	~~144~~ 153	783	
Great Carrs	~~144~~ 154	785	
Great End	~~144~~ 155	910	
Green Crag	~~144~~ 156	488	
Grey Friar	~~144~~ 156	770	
Hard Knott	~~144~~ 157	549	
Harter Fell	~~144~~ 157	653	4:5:05
Holme Fell	~~144~~ 158	317	
Ill Crag	~~144~~ 158	935	9.9.97
Illgill Head	~~144~~ 159	609	
Lingmell	~~144~~ 160	800	
Lingmoor Fell	~~144~~ 160	469	
Little Stand	~~144~~ 161	740	
Pike of Blisco	~~144~~ 161	705	6.9.99
Rossett Pike	~~144~~ 162	651	9.9.99
Rosthwaite Fell	~~144~~ 163	612	
Scafell	~~144~~ 164	964	
Scafell Pike	~~144~~ 165	978	9.9.97
Seathwaite Fell	~~144~~ 166	632	
Slight Side	~~144~~ 166	762	
Swirl How	~~144~~ 167	802	11:5:05
Walna Scar	~~144~~ 167	621	11:5:05
Weatherlam	~~144~~ 168	763	11:5:05
Whin Rigg	~~144~~ 168	535	
White Maiden	~~144~~ 169	610	
Whitfell	~~144~~ 169	573	

Allen Crags 785m 2576' NGR NY278085
237

Landranger 89 & 90   Outdoor Leisure 4 & 6

Route from				Ascent	Km	Time
Seathwaite via:						
Grains and Allen Gills				655	4.0	
Grains and Ruddy Gills				655	4.25	

Ridge routes				Descent	Ascent	Km
Esk Pike				130	30	1.25
Glaramara				108	9	2.5
Great End				155	30	1.75
Rossett Pike				91	225	2.0

Features visited			
Summit cairn			
High House Tarn top #			
Red Beck top (721m) *			
High House Tarn			
Lincomb Tarns			

Notes _____
_____
_____
_____
_____
_____
_____
_____

Times and Weather			
Departure time			
Arrival time			
Duration			
Weather			
Visibility			

_____
_____

Features details: # = located at (684m) G.R. 240092, * = located at G.R. 243097.

Black Fell CRAG. 322m 1056' NGR NY340016

Landranger 90   Outdoor Leisure 7

Route from				Ascent	Km	Time
From Coniston Road @:						
Park Fell (335029)				212	2.75	
Hollin Bank (330023)				177	2.25	
Tarn Hows car park				122c	3.5c	

Features visited			
O.S. trig. point			
North top (284m)			
South East cairn			

Notes _____
_____
_____
_____
_____

Times and Weather			
Departure time			
Arrival time			
Duration			
Weather			
Visibility			

_____
_____
_____
_____
_____

Black Sails   745m   2444'   NGR NY283008
Landranger 89 & 90   Outdoor Leisure 6

Route from	11.5.05			Ascent	Km	Time
Coniston via Swirl Hause				690	5.25	

Ridge routes				Descent	Ascent	Km
Swirl How	P.167	FROM		177	120	1.25
Weatherlam	P.168	ONTO		62	45	.75

Features visited			
Summit cairn	✻	NO	
O.S. trig. point		NO	

Times and Weather			
Departure time	?		
Arrival time	?		
Duration	?		
Weather	SUNNY WARM		
Visibility	V. GOOD		

Notes   ✻ We didn't summit, but walked along the Northern flanks (700 metres above sea level)

Bowfell 902m 2959' NGR NY245064

Landranger 89 & 90 Outdoor Leisure 6

Route from/via	9-9-99			Ascent	Km	Time
Brotherilkeld/Three Tarns				802	7.0	
Brotherilkeld/Ore Gap				802	8.25	
Cockley Beck Bridge 1				682	6.25	
Cockley Beck Bridge 2				682	7.5	
Dungeon Ghyll c.p.* via:						
The Band				812	5.75	
Hell Gill				812	6.0	
Mickleden - direct				812	6.0	
Mickleden & Rossett Gap				812	7.0	
Stonethwaite/Langstrath				802	10.0c	
Stonethwaite/Stake Pass				802	10.0c	

Ridge routes				Descent	Ascent	Km
Esk Pike P.152	FROM			115	132	1.5
Crinkle Crags P.150	ONTO			84	127	2.0
Rossett Pike				41	292	1.5

Features visited		
Summit cairn	YES	
O.S. trig. point		
North top (886m)	YES	
Three Tarns	YES	
Bowfell Buttress	YES	
Cambridge Crag		
Great Slab (Flat Crags)	YES	
Whorneyside Force		

Times and Weather		
Departure time	12:09	
Arrival time	12:42	
Duration	33 MINS	
Weather	DRY, COLD V.WINDY	
Visibility	V.GOOD	

Notes _____

_____
_____
_____
_____
_____
_____
_____

Route details: 1 = via Three Tarns 2 = via Ore Gap. # = from main car park @ G.R. 294063,
Deduct 1Km. for a start from the Old Dungeon Ghyll Hotel.

Brim Fell   796m   2612'   NGR SD271985

Landranger 96   Outdoor Leisure 6

Route from/via	11-5-05			Ascent	Km	Time
Coniston Levers Water #				741	4.75	
Coniston via Low Water				741	3.74	
Hinning House Close c.p. *				546	5.0	

Ridge routes				Descent	Ascent	Km
Dow Crag				129	147	1.25
The Old Man of Coniston	P149 FROM			28	21	.75
Swirl How	P.167 ONTO			13	11	2.0

Features visited			
Summit cairn	YES		
Levers Water	NO		
Low Water	NO		
Seathwaite Tarn	NO		

Times and Weather			
Departure time	?		
Arrival time	?		
Duration	?		
Weather	SUNNY WARM		
Visibility	V-GOOD		

Notes _____

_____
_____
_____
_____
_____
_____
_____
_____
_____
_____
_____
_____
_____

Broad Crag   934m   3064'   NGR NY219075
Landranger 89 & 90   Outdoor Leisure 6

Route from	9-9-97			Ascent	Km	Time
Brotherilkeld				840	8.25	
Wasdale Head				854	4.75	
SEATHWAITE	ASCENT					

Ridge routes				Descent	Ascent	Km
Esk Pike				130	179	2.25
Great End				65	89	1.25
Ill Crag	P. 158	FROM		50	49	.75
Lingmell				60	194	1.5
Scafell Pike	P.165	ONTO		63	19	.5

Features visited				Notes
Summit cairn	YES			
Middleboot Knotts (703m)	NO			

Times and Weather			
Departure time	?		
Arrival time	?		
Duration	?		
Weather	HOT/SUNNY		
Visibility	V.GOOD		

Brown Pike   682m   2238'   NGR SD260966
Landranger 96   Outdoor Leisure 6

Route from	11-5.05			Ascent	Km	Time
Torver				577	5.0	
Turner Hall Farm (233964)				532	3.25	

Ridge routes				Descent	Ascent	Km
Buck Pike	P. 148	ONTO		62	nil	.5
Walna Scar	P. 167	FROM		26	87	.25

Features visited				Notes
Summit cairn	YES			
Blind Tarn	NO			

Times and Weather			
Departure time	?		
Arrival time	?		
Duration	?		
Weather	SUNNY WARM		
Visibility	V.GOOD		

Buck Pike   744m   2441'   NGR SD262972
Landranger 96   Outdoor Leisure 6

Route from	*11·5·05*			Ascent	Km	Time

Ridge routes				Descent	Ascent	Km
Brown Pike	*P.147*	*FROM*		nil	62	.5
Dow Crag	*P.151*	*ONTO*		34	nil	.5

Features visited			
Summit cairn	*YES*		

Notes _____

Times and Weather			
Departure time	*?*		
Arrival time	*?*		
Duration	*?*		
Weather	*SUNNY WARM*		
Visibility	*V.GOOD*		

Cold Pike   701m   2300'   NGR NY263036
Landranger 89 & 90   Outdoor Leisure 6

Route from				Ascent	Km	Time
Cockley Beck Bridge				481	4.75	
Wrynose Bottom (266023)				431	4.5	
Wrynose Pass, Three Shire Stone				308	1.75	

Ridge routes				Descent	Ascent	Km
Crinkle Crags				214	56	2.0
Little Stand				82	56	2.25
Pike of Blisco				180	176	1.5

Features visited			
Summit cairn			
O.S. trig. point			
W top cairn (683m) (259036)			
Far W. top (670m) (256037)			

Notes _____

Times and Weather			
Departure time			
Arrival time			
Duration			
Weather			
Visibility			

The Old Man of Coniston   803m   2635' NGR SD272978
Landranger 96   Outdoor Leisure 6

Route from	1-5-02	11-5-05		Ascent	Km	Time
Coniston via:						
Boo Tarn #				748	3.75c	
Cove hut and quarries				748	4.75	
Goats Hause ∝ *BOO TARN* ✳ DESCENT				748	6.25	2 HRS
Low Water ∝ *BIG HILL* ✳ ASCENT				748	3.5	
Hinning House Close c. p. *				593	5.5	
Torver via						
Cove hut and quarries				698	5.0	
Goats Hause				698	6.25	

Ridge routes				Descent	Ascent	Km
Brim fell P.146		ONTO		21	28	.75
Dow Crag P.151		FROM		129	154	1.5

Features visited			
Summit cairn	YES	YES	
O.S. trig. point	YES	NO	
Goat Water	DESCENT	NO	
Low Water	ASCENT	NO	
Seathwaite Tarn	NO	NO	

Times and Weather			
Departure time	10:40	?	
Arrival time	12:30	?	
Duration	1H.50M	?	
Weather	V. POOR	SUNNY WARM	
Visibility	V. POOR	V. GOOD	

Notes ✳ *from/To Car park @ 288970*
*1-5-02 = MY 42nd BIRTHDAY!! This walk would've
encompassed DOW Crag, BUCK Pike and Brown Pike
if the weather had been better. It was very cold
& windy with heavy showers – hail on the top.*

Route details: # = via Boo Tarn and Bursting Stone Quarry, * = from G. R.236995.

Crinkle Crags   859m   2818'   NGR NY249049
Landranger 89 & 90   Outdoor Leisure 6

Route from	6-9-99	9-9-99		Ascent	Km	Time	
Brotherilkeld via:							
Adam-a-Crag				765	6.0		
Three Tarns				765	7.5		
Cockley Beck Bridge				639	3.5		
Dungeon Ghyll c. p. via:							
Hell Ghyll & Three Tarns				769	6.25		
Red Tarn		DESCENT		769	6.0	2 HRS	(from Crag
The Band & Three Tarns				769	6.0		
Whorney side - direct				769	5.0		
Wrynose Pass, Three shire stone				466	3.5		
* C.B. Bridge & Wrynose DESCENT							

Ridge routes				Descent	Ascent	Km
Bowfell P.145		FROM		127	84	2.0
Cold Pike				56	214	2.0
Little Stand				30	149	1.75
Pike of Blisco P.161	FROM			180	334	2.5

Features visited			
Summit cairn	NO	YES	
South top (834m) (250046)	YES	YES	
Great Knott (696m) (260043)*	NO	YES	
Shelter Crag (815m) (250053)	NO	YES	
The Bad Step	YES	NO	
Red Tarn	YES	YES	
Three Tarns	NO	YES	
Whorneyside Force	NO	NO	

Times and Weather			
Departure time	?	13:10	
Arrival time Crag No.5	?	14:00	
Duration	?	50mins	
Weather	FOG	DRY, COLD V.WINDY	
Visibility	V.POOR	V.GOOD	

Notes *6-9-99. Had to descend with compass due to virtually zero visibility - chose to go South West because of difficult terrain to the North and East. From Cockley Bridge had to walk back to Dungeon Ghyll via Wrynose Pass Blea Tarn and Wall End - MUST DO THESE CRAGS AGAIN ON FINE DAY

Route details: * = Not part of Crinkle Crags, but separate using the criteria of 15m of re-ascent on all sides. Practically it can be considered as part of the Crinkle Crags group.

Dow Crag   778m   788m   2553'   NGR SD262978

(handwritten: 778m, 978)

Landranger 96   Outdoor Leisure 6

Route from/via	11-5-05			Ascent	Km	Time
Coniston/Goats Water/direct				723	5.0	
Coniston/Goats Hause				723	6.0	
Hinning House Close c.p. #				568	5.25	
Torver/Goats Water/direct				673	4.74	
Torver/Goats Hause				673	5.5	

Ridge routes				Descent	Ascent	Km
Buck Pike P.148 FROM				nil	34	.5
Brim Fell				147	129	1.25
The Old Man of Coniston P.149 ONTO				154	129	1.5

Features visited			
Summit cairn	YES		
Goats Water	NO		
Seathwaite Tarn	NO		

Times and Weather			
Departure time	?		
Arrival time	?		
Duration	?		
Weather	SUNNY WARM		
Visibility	V.GOOD		

Notes _____

_____

_____

_____

_____

_____

_____

_____

_____

_____

Route details: # = from G. R. 236995.

Esk Pike   885m   2904'   NGR NY~~273~~075 *237*
Landranger 89 & 90   Outdoor Leisure 6

Route from/via	9.9.99			Ascent	Km	Time
Brotherilkeld/Esk Hause				791	9.0c	
Brotherilkeld/Ore Gap				791	7.75	
Dungeon Ghyll/Esk Hause				795	7.5c	
Dungeon Ghyll/Ore Gap				795	7.25c	
Seathwaite via Grains Gill				755	5.0c	
Seathwaite via Styhead Gill				755	6.25c	
Wasdale Head/Styhead				805	6.0	

Ridge routes				Descent	Ascent	Km
Allen Crags				30	130	1.25
Bowfell P.145 ONTO				132	115	1.5
Broad Crag				179	130	2.25
Great End				155	130	1.75
Ill Crag				180	130	2.25
Rossett Pike P.162 FROM				41	275	2.25

Features visited		
Summit cairn	YES	
Angle tarn	YES	
Sprinkling Tarn	NO	
Styhead Tarn	NO	

Times and Weather		
Departure time	10:46	
Arrival time	12:07	
Duration	1hr 21mins	
Weather	DRY, COLD V. WINDY	
Visibility	V. GOOD	

Notes _____
_____
_____
_____
_____
_____
_____
_____
_____
_____
_____
_____

Glaramara   783m   2569'   NGR NY246105
Landranger 89 & 90   Outdoor Leisure 4 & 6

Route from/via				Ascent	Km	Time
Seathwaite #				653	3.75	
Seatoller via North ridge				663	4.5	
Seatoller via Comb Door				663	4.5	
Stonethwaite/South Crag				683	6.0c	

Ridge routes				Descent	Ascent	Km
Allen Crags				9	108	2.5
Rosthwaite Fell				52 *	223 *	2.0

Features visited			
Summit cairns			
Combe Door top (676m) 1			
Combe Head (735m) 2			
Looking Steads top (775m) 3			
Red Beck top (721m) 4			
High House Tarns			
Lincomb Tarns			

Times and Weather			
Departure time			
Arrival time			
Duration			
Weather			
Visibility			

Notes _____

_____

_____

_____

_____

_____

_____

_____

_____

_____

_____

Route details: # = via North West flank (Hind Gill), * = approximate depending on route.
Feature details: 1= G. R. 253109, 2 = G. R. 250109, 3 = G.R. 246102, 4 = G.R. 243097.

Great Carrs   785m 2576' NGR NY270009
Landranger 89 & 90 Outdoor Leisure 6

Route from				Ascent	Km	Time
Little Langdale (316034) and:						
Greenburn Beck #				695	5.5	
High End/Rough Crags				695	6.0	
Three Shire Stone				392	2.0	

Ridge routes				Descent	Ascent	Km
Grey Friar				75	90	1.25
Swirl How				37	20	.5

Features visited			
Summit stones			
Greenburn Reservoir			
Hell Gill Pike (692m)			
Little Carrs			
Memorial Cross			
Aeroplane wreckage			

Times and Weather			
Departure time			
Arrival time			
Duration			
Weather			
Visibility			

Notes _____

Route details: # = via Broad Slack.

Great End   910m   2986'   NGR NY227084
Landranger 89 & 90   Outdoor Leisure 6

Route from/via				Ascent	Km	Time
Dungeon Ghyll car park				820	8.25	
Seathwaite/Corridor Route				780	6.0	
Seathwaite/via Esk Hause				780	5.5	
Wasdale Head/Corridor route				830	5.75	

Ridge routes				Descent	Ascent	Km
Allen Crags				30	155	1.75
Broad Crag				89	65	1.25
Esk Pike				130	155	1.75
Ill Crag				90	65	1.25
Scafell Pike				133	65	1.75

Features visited			
Summit cairn			
Round How (741m)			
Cust's Gully			
Sprinkling Tarn			
Styhead Tarn			
Lambsfoot Dub			

Times and Weather			
Departure time			
Arrival time			
Duration			
Weather			
Visibility			

Notes _____

_____

_____

_____

_____

_____

_____

_____

_____

_____

Green Crag   488m   1604'   NGR SD200983
(Ulpha Fell) Landranger 96   Outdoor Leisure 6

Route from				Ascent	Km	Time
Grassguards (224981)				254	3.0	
Eskdale (Woolpack Inn)				409	3.5	

Ridge routes				Descent	Ascent	Km
Harter Fell				304	144	2.5

Features visited				Notes
Summit cairn				

Times and Weather			
Departure time			
Arrival time			
Duration			
Weather			
Visibility			

Grey Friar   770m   2526'   NGR NY260004
Landranger 89 & 90   Outdoor Leisure 6

Route from				Ascent	Km	Time
Cockley Beck Bridge				550	2.0	
Hinning House Close c. p.#				560	3.5c	
Three Shire Stone *				377	2.75	
Wrynose Bottom 1				550	1.75	

Ridge routes				Descent	Ascent	Km
Great Carrs				90	75	1.25
Swirl How				107	75	1.5

Features visited			
Summit cairn			

Times and Weather			
Departure time			
Arrival time			
Duration			
Weather			
Visibility			

Notes

Route details: # = from G. R.
236995, * = avoiding Great
Carrs, 1 = via Troughton Gill.

Hard Knott   549m   1801'   NGR NY232024
Landranger 89 & 90   Outdoor Leisure 6

Route from				Ascent	Km	Time
Hardknott Pass (232014)				156	1.0	

Features visited				Notes _____
Summit cairn				
Eskdale Needle				
Border End (522m)				
Yew bank (499m)				
Hardknott Fort				

Times and Weather			
Departure time			
Arrival time			
Duration			
Weather			
Visibility			

Harter Fell   653m   2142'   NGR SD219997
Landranger 89 & 96   Outdoor Leisure 6

Route from	4-5-05			Ascent	Km	Time
Brotherilkeld				559	3.0	
Hardknott Pass (232014) ASCENT + DESCENT				260	2.25	5'50"
Hinning House Close c. p. #				443	2.25	
Woolpack Inn *				573	3.5	

Ridge routes				Descent	Ascent	Km
Green Crag	NO			144	304	2.5

Features visited				Notes * Had a hour
Summit cairn	YES			for lunch + sun-
O.S. trig. point	YES			bathing on way up.

Also birding en-
route.

Times and Weather			
Departure time	11:00		
Arrival time ✳	14:05		
Duration	3'05"		
Weather	V. GOOD		
Visibility	V. GOOD		

Route details: # = from G. R.
232014, * from G. R. 236995
at Wha House Bridge.

Holme Fell   317m   1040'   NGR NY315005
Landranger 90   Outdoor Leisure 6 & 7

Route from			Ascent	Km	Time
High Tilberthwaite			167	1.5	
Hodge Close			177	1.5	
Low Tilberthwaite car park			167	2.0	
Yew Tree Farm			220	1.75	

Features visited				Notes _____
Summit cairn				
Summit tarns				
Ivy Crag cairn				
Yew Tree Tarn				
Hodge Close Quarries				

Times and Weather			
Departure time			
Arrival time			
Duration			
Weather			
Visibility			

Ill Crag   935m   3068'   NGR NY223073
Landranger 89 & 90   Outdoor Leisure 6

Route from	9-9-97		Ascent	Km	Time
Brotherilkeld			841	8.5	
Wasdale Head/corridor route			855	6.5	
SEATHWAITE via ESK HAUSE ASCENT					

Ridge routes			Descent	Ascent	Km
Broad Crag P.147	ONTO		49	50	.75
Esk Pike			130	180	2.25
Great End			65	90	1.25
Scafell Pike	ONTO		63	20	1.0
Lingmell			60	195	2.0

Features visited				Notes ✶ We didn't
Summit cairn	✶ NO			Summit but
				Walked along the
				N W flank at
				900 metres above

Times and Weather				Sea Level.
Departure time				
Arrival time				
Duration				
Weather	SUNNY			
Visibility	V.GooD			

Illgill Head   609m   1998'   NGR NY169049
(Wastwater Screes) Landranger 89   Outdoor Leisure 6

Route from				Ascent	Km	Time
Boot				549	6.25	
Brackenclose car park				539	3.25	
Eskdale Green				559	9.0	
Wasdale Head				529	4.75	
Woolpack Inn				529	7.75	

Ridge routes				Descent	Ascent	Km
Whin Rigg				60	134	2.5

Features visited			
Summit cairn			
O.S. trig. point			
Burnmoor Tarn			
Stone Circle (Brat's Moss)			

Times and Weather			
Departure time			
Arrival time			
Duration			
Weather			
Visibility			

Notes _____

_____
_____
_____
_____
_____
_____
_____
_____
_____
_____

Lingmell   800m   2625'   NGR NY209082
Landranger 89 & 90   Outdoor Leisure 6

Route from/via				Ascent	Km	Time
Seathwaite/Corridor Route				670	6.25	
Wasdale Head via:						
Brown Tongue				720	4.25	
S. W. ridge (The Shoulder)				720	3.5	

Ridge routes				Descent	Ascent	Km
Broad Crag				194	60	1.5
Ill Crag				195	60	2.0
Scafell Pike				238	60	1.25

Features visited				Notes _____
Summit cairn				_____
				_____

Times and Weather				_____
Departure time				_____
Arrival time				_____
Duration				_____
Weather				_____
Visibility				_____

Lingmoor Fell   469m   1539'   NGR NY303146 046
Landranger 90   Outdoor Leisure 6 & 7

Route from				Ascent	Km	Time
Blea Tarn car park				114	1.5	
Chapel Stile				379	4.0c	
Dungeon Ghyll car park				379	3.75c	
Elterwater				399	3.75c	
Little Langdale				379	2.5	

Features visited				Notes _____
Summit cairn				_____
Side Pike				_____
Oak How Needle				_____
				_____

Times and Weather				_____
Departure time				_____
Arrival time				_____
Duration				_____
Weather				_____
Visibility				_____

Little Stand 740m 2428' NGR NY250034
Landranger 89 & 90 Outdoor Leisure 6

Route from				Ascent	Km	Time
Cockley Beck Bridge				520	2.0	
Wrynose Bottom				450	2.75	

Ridge routes				Descent	Ascent	Km
Cold Pike				56	82	2.25
Crinkle Crags				149	30	1.75

Features visited			
Summit cairn			
O.S. trig. point			

Times and Weather			
Departure time			
Arrival time			
Duration			
Weather			
Visibility			

Notes _____

Pike of Blisco 705m 2313' NGR NY271042
Landranger 89 & 90 Outdoor Leisure 6

Route from	6-9-99			Ascent	Km	Time
Dungeon Ghyll via:						
Stool End Farm				615	5.0	
Wall End & Redacre Gill				615	4.0	
Three Shire stone				312	1.75	
Wrynose Bridge				425	1.5	
SIDE PIKE	ASCENT					

Ridge routes				Descent	Ascent	Km
Cold Pike				176	180	1.5
Crinkle Crags	ONTO			334	180	2.5

Features visited			
Summit cairn	YES		
Red Tarn	YES		

Times and Weather			
Departure time Green House	11:00		
Arrival time	13:00		
Duration	2 HRS		
Weather	WARM SUNNY		
Visibility ✳	GOOD		

Notes ✳ The first 2 crinkle crags were visited, but the weather deteriorated and we were forced to descend; and ended up in Wrynose !!

Rossett Pike   651m   2136' NGR NY249076
Landranger 89 & 90   Outdoor Leisure 6

Route from	9-9-99			Ascent	Km	Time
Dungeon Ghyll c. p. via:						
Stake Gill				561	7.5c	
Rossett Gill	ASCENT			561	6.0c	

Ridge routes				Descent	Ascent	Km
Southern Fells						
Allen Crags				225	91	2.0
Bowfell				292	41	1.5
Esk Pike P.152	ONTO			275	41	2.25
Central Fells						
Harrison Stickle				251	166c	4.5
High Raise				277	166c	4.0
Loft Crag				185	166c	4.5
Pike of Stickle				224	166c	4.0
Thurnacar Knott				238	166c	4.25

Features visited			
Summit cairn	YES		

Times and Weather			
Departure time			
Arrival time	10;40		
Duration			
Weather ✳	D.C.W		
Visibility	GOOD		

Notes ✳ D = Dry   C = Cold   W = Windy

Rosthwaite Fell   612m   2008'   NGR NY256118
Landranger 89 & 90   Outdoor Leisure 4

Route from/via				Ascent	Km	Time
Seatoller				492	3.0	
Stonethwaite/Stanger Gill				512	2.5	

Ridge routes				Descent	Ascent	Km
Glaramara				223 #	52 #	2.0 #

Features visited			
Summit cairn (Rosth. Cam)			
Bessyboot O.S. trig. point			
Dovenest top (632m) 1			
Combe Door top (676m) 2			
Combe Head (735m) 3			
Tarn at Leaves			

Times and Weather			
Departure time			
Arrival time			
Duration			
Weather			
Visibility			

Notes _____

_____
_____
_____
_____
_____
_____
_____
_____
_____
_____

Route details: # = very approximate depending on route. 1 = G.R. 256114, 2 = G.R. 253109, 3 = G. R. 250109.

Scafell   964m   3163'   NGR NY207065
Landranger 89 & 90 Outdoor Leisure 6

Route from				Ascent	Km	Time
Boot via Burnmoor Tarn				904	6.5	
Brotherilkeld #				870	7.0 - 7.75	
Wasdale Head via:						
Brown Tongue/L.Rake *				884	4.0	
Green How				884	5.0	

Ridge routes				Descent	Ascent	Km
Scafell Pike 1				227c	214c	1.0 - 2.0
Slight Side				nil	202	1.5

Features visited			
Summit cairn			
Summit Shelter			
Broad Stand			
Foxes Tarn			

Times and Weather			
Departure time			
Arrival time			
Duration			
Weather			
Visibility			

Notes _____
_____
_____
_____
_____
_____
_____
_____
_____
_____
_____

Route details: # = There are 4 routes via Cam Spout 1= via Foxes Tarn, 2 = via Lord's Rake, 3 = via Cam Spout Crags, 4 = via Broad Stand. Note the appropriate number above. * = when starting from Brackenclose add 10m ascent and reduce distance by .5Km.
Ridge Route Details: 1 = There are 5 ridge paths from Scafell Pike: A= via Broad Stand, B = via Foxes Tarn, C = via Lord's Rake, D = via Mickledore Chimney, E = via West Wall Traverse. Note the appropriate letter above.

Scafell Pike   978m   3208'   NGR NY215072
Landranger 89 & 90   Outdoor Leisure 6

Route from				Ascent	Km	Time
	9-9-97					
Wasdale Head via:						
Corridor Route				898	6.5	
Piers Gill				898	5.0	
Hollow Stones				898	4.5c	
Brotherilkeld via:						
How Beck				884	7.75	
Little Narrowcove				884	8.25	
Seathwaite via:						
Corridor Route ✳	DESCENT			848	6.5	
Esk Hause	ASCENT			848	6.25	

Ridge routes				Descent	Ascent	Km
Broad Crag P.147	YES			19	63	.5
Great End	NO			65	133	1.75
Ill Crag	NO			20	63	1.0
Lingmell	NO			60	238	1.25
Scafell P.	NO			214c	227c	1.0 - 2.0

Features visited			
Summit cairn	YES		
O.S. trig. point	YES		
Summit shelter	YES		

Times and Weather			
Departure time	?		
Arrival time	?		
Duration	?		
Weather	SUNNY		
Visibility	V.GOOD		

Notes   ✳ Although we descended via the Corridor Route, we didn't descend all the way to Seathwaite immediately — we went on to Great and Green Gable (P.177 & P.178)

Seathwaite Fell   632m   2074'   NGR NY227097
Landranger 89 & 90   Outdoor Leisure 4 & 6

Route from				Ascent	Km	Time
Seathwaite				502	3.25	

Features visited				Notes _____
Summit cairn				_____
O.S. trig. point				_____
South top (631m) (228094)				_____
Sprinkling Tarn				_____
Styhead Tarn				_____
				_____

Times and Weather				_____
Departure time				_____
Arrival time				_____
Duration				_____
Weather				_____
Visibility				_____

Slight Side   762m   2500'   NGR NY209051
Landranger 90   Outdoor Leisure 6

Route from				Ascent	Km	Time
Boot				702	6.0	
Wha House Farm				702	4.75	

Ridge routes				Descent	Ascent	Km
Scafell				202	nil	1.5

Features visited				Notes _____
Summit cairn				_____
				_____

Times and Weather				_____
Departure time				_____
Arrival time				Route details: This fell is
Duration				strictly the southern extension
Weather				of the Scafell ridge. Height is
Visibility				marked as 748m on 1:25 000

Ordnance Survey map.

Swirl How   802m   2631'   NGR NY273005
Landranger 89 & 90   Outdoor Leisure 6

Route from/via	*11-5-05*			Ascent	Km	Time
Coniston via Swirl Hause				747	5.0	
Coniston via Levers Hause				747	5.25	
Little Langdale/Swirl Hause				712	5.75	

Ridge routes				Descent	Ascent	Km
Black Sails	*P.144*	*ONTO*		120	177	1.25
Brim Fell	*P.146*	*FROM*		11	13	2.0
Great Carrs				20	37	.5
Grey Friar				75	107	1.5
Weatherlam				137	177	1.75

Features visited			Notes _____
Summit cairn	*YES*		

Notes _____
_____

Times and Weather		
Departure time	*?*	
Arrival time	*?*	
Duration	*?*	
Weather	*SUNNY WARM*	
Visibility	*V. GOOD*	

Walna Scar   621m   2038'   NGR SD258963
Landranger 96   Outdoor Leisure 6

Route from	*11-5-05*			Ascent	Km	Time
Torver				516	4.5	
Turner Hall Farm				471	3.25	
Car Park at 288970	*ASCENT*					

Ridge routes				Descent	Ascent	Km
Brown Pike	*P147*	*ONTO*		87	26	.5
White Maiden				23	36	.75

Features visited		
Summit cairn	*✳*	*NO*

Notes ✳ We didn't
Summit but
Skirted the N.E
flank @ 610 metres
above sea level.

Times and Weather		
Departure time	*?*	
Arrival time	*?*	
Duration	*?*	
Weather	*SUNNY WARM*	
Visibility	*V. GOOD*	

Weatherlam   763m   2503'   NGR NY288011
Landranger 89   Outdoor Leisure 6

Route from	_11.505_			Ascent	Km	Time
Coniston via Lad Stones	_DESCENT_			708	4.25	
Coniston via Red Dell Beck				708	4.5	
Little Langdale				673	4.0	
Low Tilberthwaite				613	3.5	

Ridge routes				Descent	Ascent	Km
Black Sails	_FROM_			45	62	.75
Swirl How				177	137	1.75

Features visited			
Summit cairn	_YES_		
O.S. trig. point	_NO_		

Times and Weather			
Departure time	_?._		
Arrival time	_?._		
Duration	_?._		
Weather	_SUNNY WARM_		
Visibility	_V.GOOD_		

Notes _____
_____
_____
_____
_____
_____
_____
_____
_____
_____
_____

Whin Rigg   535m   1755'   NGR NY152034
Landranger 89   Outdoor Leisure 6

Route from				Ascent	Km	Time
Eskdale Green				485	4.75	
Nether Wasdale				480	3.75	

Ridge routes				Descent	Ascent	Km
Illgill Head				134	60	2.5

Features visited			
Summit cairn			

Times and Weather			
Departure time			
Arrival time			
Duration			
Weather			
Visibility			

Notes _____
_____
_____
_____
_____
_____
_____
_____
_____

White Maiden   610m   2001'   NGR SD254957
Landranger 96   Outdoor Leisure 6

Route from				Ascent	Km	Time
Turner Hall Farm 233964				460	3.25	

Ridge routes				Descent	Ascent	Km
Walna Scar				36	23	.75

Features visited			
Summit cairn			
White Pike (598m) (249955)			

Times and Weather			
Departure time			
Arrival time			
Duration			
Weather			
Visibility			

Notes _____
_____
_____
_____
_____
_____
_____
_____
_____
_____
_____

Whitfell   573m   1880'   NGR SD158930
Landranger 96   Outdoor Leisure 6

Route from				Ascent	Km	Time
Ulpha				493	4.75	
Waberthwaite				537	5.75	

Features visited			
Summit cairn			
O.S. trig. point			

Times and Weather			
Departure time			
Arrival time			
Duration			
Weather			
Visibility			

Notes _____
_____
_____
_____
_____
_____
_____
_____
_____
_____
_____

CHAPTER NINE

WESTERN LAKE DISTRICT

Mountain	Page	Height in Metres	Date first Ascended
Base Brown	171	646	___:___:___
Black Crag	171	828	___:___:___
Blake Fell	172	573	___:___:___
Brandreth	172	715	4:9:97
Buckbarrow	173	400	___:___:___
Burnbank Fell	173	475	___:___:___
Caw Fell	174	690	___:___:___
Crag Fell	174	523	___:___:___
Fellbarrow	175	416	___:___:___
Fleetwith Pike	175	648	8:9:00
Gavel Fell	176	526	___:___:___
Great Borne	176	616	___:___:___
Great Gable	177	899	9:9:97
Green Gable	178	801	9:9:97
Grey Knotts	179	697	4:9:97
Grike	179	488	___:___:___
Haycock	180	797	___:___:___
Haystacks	181	597	11:9:97
Hen Comb	182	509	___:___:___
High Crag	182	744	2:9:97
High Stile	183	807	2:9:97
Iron Crag	183	640	___:___:___
Kirk Fell	184	802	___:___:___
Lank Rigg	185	541	___:___:___
Low Fell	185	423	___:___:___
Mellbreak	186	512	___:___:___
Middle Fell	186	582	___:___:___
Pillar	187	892	___:___:___
Red Pike, Buttermere	188	755	2:9:97
Red Pike, Wasdale	189	826	___:___:___
Scoat Fell	189	841	___:___:___
Seatallan	190	693	___:___:___
Starling Dodd	190	633	___:___:___
Steeple	191	819	___:___:___
Whoap	191	511	___:___:___
Yewbarrow	192	628	___:___:___

Base Brown   646m   2120'   NGR NY225115
Landranger 89 & 90   Outdoor Leisure 4

Route from				Ascent	Km	Time
Seathwaite				516	1.75 - 2.5	

Ridge routes				Descent	Ascent	Km
Green Gable				196	41	1.4

Features visited				Notes _____
Summit cairn				
Hanging Stone				

Times and Weather			
Departure time			
Arrival time			
Duration			
Weather			
Visibility			

Black Crag   828m   2717'   NGR NY166116
Landranger 89   Outdoor Leisure 4 & 6

Route from/via				Ascent	Km	Time
Wasdale Head/Wind Gap				748	4.0	

Ridge routes				Descent	Ascent	Km
Pillar				87	23	.75
Scoat Fell				46	33	.5

Features visited				Notes _____
Summit cairn				

Times and Weather			
Departure time			
Arrival time			
Duration			
Weather			
Visibility			

Blake Fell   573m   1880'   NGR NY111196
Landranger 89   Outdoor Leisure 4

Route from				Ascent	Km	Time
Lamplugh				383	3.25	
Loweswater				463	4.0	

Ridge routes				Descent	Ascent	Km
Burnbank Fell				20	118	1.5
Gavel Fell				71	118	1.5

Features visited			
Summit cairn			

Times and Weather			
Departure time			
Arrival time			
Duration			
Weather			
Visibility			

Notes _____
_____
_____
_____
_____
_____
_____
_____
_____
_____
_____

Brandreth   715m   236'   NGR NY215119
Landranger 89 & 90   Outdoor Leisure 4

Route from	49.97			Ascent	Km	Time
Black Sail y.h. via Loft Beck				425	2.5	
Gatesgarth				595	4.0c	
Honister Hause	ASCENT			515	2.75	
Seathwaite #				585	2.75	

Ridge routes				Descent	Ascent	Km
Green Gable				106	20	1.25
Grey Knotts	ONTO			17	35	1.0
Fleetwith Pike				113	180	3.5
Haystacks				103	221	3.0

Features visited			
Summit cairn	YES		

Times and Weather			
Departure time	?		
Arrival time	?		
Duration	?		
Weather	DRIZZLE		
Visibility	V. POOR		

Notes Had intended
to climb Great
Gable but for
safety's sake
turned back
due to poor
visibility

Route details: # = via Giller-
comb Head.

Buckbarrow   400m   1312'   NGR NY136059
Landranger 89   Outdoor Leisure 6

Route from				Ascent	Km	Time
Nether Wasdale				345	2.75	

Ridge routes				Descent	Ascent	Km
Seatallan				292	nil	2.6

Features visited				Notes_____
Summits:				
Buckbarrow (400m)				
Glade How (420m)				

Times and Weather			
Departure time			
Arrival time			
Duration			
Weather			
Visibility			

Burnbank Fell   475m   1558'   NGR NY110209
Landranger 89   Outdoor Leisure 4

Route from				Ascent	Km	Time
Lamplugh				285	2.5	
Waterend				335	3.25c	

Ridge routes				Descent	Ascent	Km
Blake Fell				118	20	1.5

Features visited				Notes _____
Summit				
Owsen Fell (409m)				

Times and Weather			
Departure time			
Arrival time			
Duration			
Weather			
Visibility			

122

Caw Fell   690m   2264'   NGR NY~~152~~109
Landranger 89   Outdoor Leisure 4 & 6

Route from				Ascent	Km	Time
Gosforth				620	10.5c	
Low Gillerthwaite				540	4.25	

Ridge routes				Descent	Ascent	Km
Crag Fell				133	285	5.25
Haycock				122	15	1.5
Iron Crag				55	105	1.75
Lank Rigg				291	440	5.0c
Whoap #				20	199	4.5c

Features visited			
Summit cairn			
Sampson's Bratful			

Times and Weather			
Departure time			
Arrival time			
Duration			
Weather			
Visibility			

Notes _____
_____
_____
_____
_____
_____
_____
_____
_____
_____
_____

Route details: # = via Iron Crag.

Crag Fell   523m   1716'   NGR NY096~~114~~ *144*
Landranger 89   Outdoor Leisure 4

Route from				Ascent	Km	Time
Bleach Green c.p. (085153)				393	2.5	
Ennerdale Bridge				421	4.0	
Low Gillerthwaite				373	6.0c	

Ridge routes				Descent	Ascent	Km
Caw Fell				285	133	5.25
Grike				37	72	1.5
Whoap				120	133	2.0

Features visited			
Summit cairn			

Times and Weather			
Departure time			
Arrival time			
Duration			
Weather			
Visibility			

Notes _____
_____
_____
_____
_____
_____
_____
_____
_____

Fellbarrow   416m   1365' NGR NY132242
Landranger 89   Outdoor Leisure 4

Route from				Ascent	Km	Time
Low Lorton				346	4.5c	
Thackthwaite				306	2.25	
Waterend				276	3.0	

Ridge routes				Descent	Ascent	Km
Low Fell				48	41	2.0

Features visited			
Summit cairn			
O.S. trig. point			

Times and Weather			
Departure time			
Arrival time			
Duration			
Weather			
Visibility			

Notes _____

Fleetwith Pike   648m   2126' NGR NY206142
Landranger 89 & 90   Outdoor Leisure 4

Route from/via	8-9-00			Ascent	Km	Time
Gatesgarth/Fleetwith Edge	ASCENT			528	1.25	
Gatesgarth via #	DESCENT			528	4.5	
Gatesgarth via *				528	4.5	
Honister Hause				348	2.1	

Ridge routes				Descent	Ascent	Km
Brandreth	NO			180	113	3.5
Grey Knotts	NO			162	113	2.5
Haystacks	NO			107	158	3.75

Features visited			
Summit cairn	YES		
Fanny Mercer's Cross	YES		

Times and Weather			
Departure time (Buttermere)	11:53		
Arrival time	13:22		
Duration			
Weather	CLOUDY WINDY		
Visibility	FAIR		

Notes _____

Route details: # = via
Warnscale Bottom and Quarry
Road, * = via grass path south
of Warnscale Beck.

Gavel Fell   526m   1726'   NGR NY117184
Landranger 98   Outdoor Leisure 4

Route from				Ascent	Km	Time
Croasdale				256	2.75	
Loweswater				416	4.5	

Ridge routes				Descent	Ascent	Km
Blake Fell				118	71	1.5
Great Borne				211	121	2.5

Features visited			
Summit cairn			

Times and Weather			
Departure time			
Arrival time			
Duration			
Weather			
Visibility			

Notes _____
_____
_____
_____
_____
_____
_____
_____
_____
_____

Great Borne   616m   2021'   NGR NY124164
(Herdus) Landranger 89   Outdoor Leisure 4

Route from				Ascent	Km	Time
Bowness Point c.p. (110153)				476	2.25	
Buttermere				504	7.0	
Loweswater				506	6.25	

Ridge routes				Descent	Ascent	Km
Gavel Fell				121	211	2.5
Hen Comb				104	211	2.5
Starling Dodd				115	98	2.0

Features visited			
Summit cairn			
O.S. trig. point			
North top			
Floutern Tarn			

Times and Weather			
Departure time			
Arrival time			
Duration			
Weather			
Visibility			

Notes _____
_____
_____
_____
_____
_____
_____
_____
_____
_____
_____
_____

Great Gable   899m   2949'   NGR NY211103
Landranger 89 & 90   Outdoor Leisure 4 & 6

Route from/via	*9-9-97*			Ascent	Km	Time
Gatesgarth/Scarth Gap Pass				900+#	6.5+	
Gatesgarth/Warnscale				779+#	6.0+	
Honister Hause/Beck Head				599	5.5	
Honister Hause/Windy Gap				599	5.0	
Seathwaite/Windy Gap				769	4.5	
Wasdale Head/Beck Head				819	3.75	
Wasdale Head/Great Napes				819	3.0	
Wasdale Head/Sty Head				819	4.5	
SEATHWAITE / SCA. PIKE	*P.165*					

Ridge routes				Descent	Ascent	Km
Green Gable	*ONTO*			51	149	.6
Kirk Fell				172	269	2.0

Special Route				Km
The Gable Girdle				5.0

Features visited			
Summit cairn & Memorial	*YES*		
Napes Needle	*NO*		
Sphinx Rock	*NO*		
Westmorland Cairn	*NO*		

Times and Weather			
Departure time	*?*		
Arrival time	*?*		
Duration	*?*		
Weather	*SUNNY*		
Visibility	*V. GOOD*		

Notes _____

_____
_____
_____
_____
_____
_____
_____
_____
_____
_____

Route details: # = ascent heights vary due to additional ascent from Ennerdale Valley.

Green Gable   801m   2628'   NGR NY215107
Landranger 89 & 90   Outdoor Leisure 4 & 6

Route from/via	9-9-97			Ascent	Km	Time
Black Sail youth Hostel				511	2.75	
Honister Hause				501	4.25	
Seathwaite/Gillercombe				671	2.75	
Seathwaite/Styhead Tarn	DESCENT			671	4.0	

Ridge routes				Descent	Ascent	Km
Base Brown				41	196	1.4
Brandreth				20	106	1.25
Great Gable	FROM			149	51	.6
Kirk Fell				172	171	2.5

Features visited			
Summit cairn	YES		

Times and Weather			
Departure time	?		
Arrival time	?		
Duration	?		
Weather	SUNNY		
Visibility	V. GOOD		

Notes _____

_____

_____

_____

_____

_____

_____

_____

_____

_____

_____

_____

Grey Knotts 697m 2228' NGR NY217126
Landranger 89 & 90 Outdoor Leisure 4

Route from/via	4-9-97			Ascent	Km	Time
Honister Hause via fence	DESCENT			397	1.2	
Honister Hause/Tramway				397	2.0	
Seathwaite				567	2.25	

Ridge routes				Descent	Ascent	Km
Brandreth	FROM			35	17	1.0
Fleetwith Pike				113	162	2.5
Haystacks				103	203	3.0c

Features visited				Notes _See Brandreth_
Summit cairn	YES			_(P.172)_
O.S. trig. point	NO			
Bankes Memorial (1752)	NO			

Times and Weather			
Departure time	?		
Arrival time	?		
Duration	?		
Weather	DRIZZLE		
Visibility	V. POOR		

Grike 488m 1601' NGR NY085140
Landranger 89 Outdoor Leisure 4

Route from				Ascent	Km	Time
Ennerdale Bridge				386	3.0	
Near Thwaites c.p. (062130)				228	3.5	

Ridge routes				Descent	Ascent	Km
Crag Fell				72	37	1.5

Features visited				Notes
Summit cairn				
Gt. Stone of Blakeley				
Kinniside Stone Circle				

Times and Weather			
Departure time			
Arrival time			
Duration			
Weather			
Visibility			

Haycock   797m   2615'   NGR NY145107
Landranger 89   Outdoor Leisure 4 & 6

Route from				Ascent	Km	Time
Low Gillerthwaite				647	4.5	
Netherbeck Bridge				727	5.75	
Overbeck Bridge car park				727	6.5	

Ridge routes				Descent	Ascent	Km
Caw Fell				15	122	1.5
Seatallan				197	302	2.5
Scoat Fell				136	92	1.75

Features visited			
Summit cairn			
Gowder Crag			
Little Gowder Crag (733m)			

Times and Weather			
Departure time			
Arrival time			
Duration			
Weather			
Visibility			

Notes _____
_____
_____
_____
_____
_____
_____
_____
_____
_____
_____
_____

Haystacks 597m 1959' NGR NY193132
Landranger 89 & 90 Outdoor Leisure 4

Route from	11-9-97			Ascent	Km	Time
Black Sail youth hostel via:						
Loft Beck				307	2.75	
Scarth Gap Pass				307	1.5	
Gatesgarth via:						
Scarth Gap Pass				477	2.75	
Warnscale & Quarry Road				477	4.25	
Warnscale & grass path #	ASCENT			477	4.0	
Honister Hause				297	3.5	
Scarth Gap → Buttermere	DESCENT					

Ridge routes				Descent	Ascent	Km
Brandreth				221	103	3.0
Fleetwith Pike				158	107	3.75
Grey Knotts				203	103	3.0c
High Crag				299	152	1.75

Features visited			
Summit cairns (2)	YES		
Blackbeck Tarn	YES		
Innominate Tarn	YES		
Summit Tarn	YES		

Times and Weather			
Departure time (BUTTERMERE)	?		
Arrival time	?		
Duration	?		
Weather	CLOUDY		
Visibility	V.GOOD		

Notes _____

_____
_____
_____
_____
_____
_____
_____
_____
_____
_____
_____
_____

Route details: # = grass path is the path south of Warnscale Beck.

Hen Comb   509m   1670'   NGR NY132181
Landranger 89   Outdoor Leisure 4

Route from				Ascent	Km	Time
Loweswater/Little Dodd				399	3.25	
Loweswater/Mosedale Beck				399	4.0	

Ridge routes				Descent	Ascent	Km
Great Borne				211	204	2.5

Features visited			
Summit cairn			

Times and Weather			
Departure time			
Arrival time			
Duration			
Weather			
Visibility			

Notes _____

High Crag   744m   2441'   NGR NY180140
Landranger 89 & 90   Outdoor Leisure 4

Route from	29-97			Ascent	Km	Time
Black Sail youth hostel				454	2.5	
Gatesgarth				624	3.5	
Low Gillerthwaite				594	6.5	
Buttermere #	ASCENT					

Ridge routes				Descent	Ascent	Km
Haystacks				152	299	1.75
High Stile P.183	ONTO			97	34	1.6

Features visited			
Summit cairn	YES		
Seat (561m)	NO		

Times and Weather			
Departure time	?		
Arrival time	?		
Duration	?		
Weather	D.C.W		
Visibility	AVGE		

Notes _____

Buttermere village/Burtness Wood/Comb Beck

High Stile 807m 1648' NGR NY170148
Landranger 89 Outdoor Leisure 4

Route from	2-9-97			Ascent	Km	Time
Buttermere				695	2.5	
Gatesgarth				687	2.75	

Ridge routes				Descent	Ascent	Km
High Crag	P.182	FROM		34	97	1.6
Red Pike	P.188	ONTO		40	92	1.5

Features visited			
Summit cairn	YES		

Times and Weather			
Departure time			
Arrival time			
Duration			
Weather	D.C.W		
Visibility	AVGE		

Notes _____
_____
_____
_____
_____
_____
_____
_____
_____
_____

Iron Crag 640m 2100' NGR NY123119
Landranger 89 Outdoor Leisure 4

Route from				Ascent	Km	Time
Haile				562	11.0	
Low Gillerthwaite				490	4.25c	

Ridge routes				Descent	Ascent	Km
Caw Fell				105	55	1.75
Whoap				20	149	2.75

Features visited			
Summit cairn			

Times and Weather			
Departure time			
Arrival time			
Duration			
Weather			
Visibility			

Notes _____
_____
_____
_____
_____
_____
_____
_____
_____
_____

Kirk Fell   802m   2636'   NGR NY195105
Landranger 89 & 90   Outdoor Leisure 4 & 6

Route from/via				Ascent	Km	Time
Black Sail youth hostel via:						
Beck Head				512	4.25	
Black Sail Pass				512	2.3	
Honister Hause/Beck Head				502+	5.5	
Wasdale Head via:						
Beck Head				722	4.0	
Black Sail Pass				722	4.25	
direct				722	2.0	

Ridge routes				Descent	Ascent	Km
Great Gable				269	172	2.0
Green Gable				171	172	2.5
Pillar				305	215	3.25

Features visited			
Summit cairn/shelter			
East top (787m)			
Kirk Fell Tarns			

Times and Weather			
Departure time			
Arrival time			
Duration			
Weather			
Visibility			

Notes _____

_____

_____

_____

_____

_____

_____

_____

_____

_____

_____

_____

Lank Rigg   541m   1775'   NGR NY092119
Landranger 89   Outdoor Leisure 4

Route from				Ascent	Km	Time
Calder Bridge				476	9.5c	
Near Thwaite c. p. (062130)				281	4.5	

Ridge routes				Descent	Ascent	Km
Caw Fell				440	291	5.0c
Whoap				81	111	1.25

Features visited			
Summit cairn			
O.S. trig. point			
Summit tumulus			

Times and Weather			
Departure time			
Arrival time			
Duration			
Weather			
Visibility			

Notes _____
_____
_____
_____
_____
_____
_____
_____
_____
_____
_____
_____

Low Fell   423m   1388'   NGR NY137226
Landranger 89   Outdoor Leisure 4

Route from				Ascent	Km	Time
Loweswater Village				313	2.5	
Thackthwaite				313	2.5	
Waterend				288	2.5c	

Ridge routes				Descent	Ascent	Km
Fellbarrow				41	48	2.0

Features visited			
Summit cairn			
South top (412m)			

Times and Weather			
Departure time			
Arrival time			
Duration			
Weather			
Visibility			

Notes _____
_____
_____
_____
_____
_____
_____
_____
_____
_____
_____

Mellbreak   511m   1699'   NGR NY148186
Landranger 89   Outdoor Leisure 4

Route from				Ascent	Km	Time
Buttermere via Scale Knott				400	4.0	
Loweswater Village via:						
Crummock path/N.E.flank				402	4.0	
Mosedale Beck/S.W.flank				402	3.25	
White Crag and North top				402	3.0	

Features visited			
Summit cairn			
North top (509m)			

Times and Weather			
Departure time			
Arrival time			
Duration			
Weather			
Visibility			

Notes _____
_____
_____
_____
_____
_____
_____
_____
_____
_____
_____
_____

Middle Fell   582m   1909'   NGR NY151072
Landranger 89   Outdoor Leisure 6

Route from				Ascent	Km	Time
Netherbeck Bridge #				512	2.0	
Wasdale (Greendale)				482	2.0	

Ridge routes				Descent	Ascent	Km
Seatallan				227	117	1.75

Features visited			
Summit cairn			

Times and Weather			
Departure time			
Arrival time			
Duration			
Weather			
Visibility			

Notes _____
_____
_____
_____
_____
_____
_____
_____
_____

Route details: # = via Goat Gill.

Pillar 892m 2927' NGR NY171121
Landranger 89 & 90 Outdoor Leisure 4 & 6

Route from/via				Ascent	Km	Time
Black Sail y.h./Wind Gap				602	3.5	
Gatesgarth via:						
Scarth Gap & Black Sail Passes				1017	7.0	
Pillar Cove				1017	6.0	
Low Gillerthwaite				742	5.75	
Wasdale Head				812	5.75	

Ridge routes				Descent	Ascent	Km
Black Crag				23	87	.75
Kirk Fell				215	305	3.25
Scoat Fell #				36	87	1.25

Features visited			
Summit cairn			
O.S. trig. point			
Summit windshelter			
Pillar Rock (780m)			
Rolinson's Cairn			
Looking Stead (627m)			

Times and Weather			
Departure time			
Arrival time			
Duration			
Weather			
Visibility			

Notes _____

_____

_____

_____

_____

_____

_____

_____

_____

_____

_____

_____

Route details: # = ignoring Black Crag.

Red Pike, Buttermere   755m   2477'   NGR NY160155
Landranger 89   Outdoor Leisure 4

Route from	2-9-97			Ascent	Km	Time
Buttermere via:						
Ling Comb + Dodd	DESCENT			643	3.25	
Lingcomb Edge				643	4.25	
Scale Force				643	5.25	
Sourmilk Gill				643	3.0c	
Low Gillerthwaite				605	2.75	

Ridge routes				Descent	Ascent	Km
High Stile P.183	FROM			92	40	1.5
Starling Dodd				52	174	2.0

Features visited			
Summit cairn/windshelter			
Dodd (641m) (164158)			
Bleaberry Tarn			
Scale Force			

Times and Weather			
Departure time			
Arrival time			
Duration			
Weather			
Visibility			

Notes _____

_____

_____

_____

_____

_____

_____

_____

_____

_____

_____

Red Pike, Wasdale 826m 2710' NGR NY165106
Landranger 89 Outdoor Leisure 4 & 6

Route from				Ascent	Km	Time
Overbeck Bridge #				819	5.0	
Wasdale Head #				746	3.5	

Ridge routes				Descent	Ascent	Km
Scoat Fell				26	6	1.2
Yewbarrow				183	381	2.5

Features visited			
Summit cairn			
North top (821m)			

Times and Weather			
Departure time			
Arrival time			
Duration			
Weather			
Visibility			

Notes_____
_____
_____
_____
_____
_____
_____
_____
_____

Route details: # = via Dore Head.

Scoat Fell 841m 2759' NGR NY160114
Landranger 89 Outdoor Leisure 4 & 6

Route from/via				Ascent	Km	Time
Netherbeck Bridge				771	7.0	
Wasdale Head/Wind Gap				761	4.5	

Ridge routes				Descent	Ascent	Km
Black Crag				33	46	.5
Haycock				92	136	1.75
Pillar				87	36	1.25
Red Pike (Wasdale)				6	26	1.2
Steeple				20	42	.75

Features visited			
Summit cairn			

Times and Weather			
Departure time			
Arrival time			
Duration			
Weather			
Visibility			

Notes _____
_____
_____
_____
_____
_____
_____
_____

Seatallan   693m   2274' NGR NY140084
Landranger 89   Outdoor Leisure 6

Route from				Ascent	Km	Time
Netherbeck Bridge				623	4.25	
Nether Wasdale/Gill Beck				638	5.0	
Nether Wasdale III Gill				638	7.0	
Wasdale (Greendale)				613	3.5	

Ridge routes				Descent	Ascent	Km
Haycock				302	197	2.5
Middle Fell				117	227	1.75

Features visited			
Summit cairn			
O.S. trig. point			
Summit tumulus			
Greendale Tarn			

Times and Weather			
Departure time			
Arrival time			
Duration			
Weather			
Visibility			

Notes _____

Starling Dodd   633m   2077' NGR NY142158
Landranger 89   Outdoor Leisure 4

Route from				Ascent	Km	Time
Buttermere				521	5.5	
Loweswater				523	6.0	
Low Gillerthwaite				483	2.5	

Ridge routes				Descent	Ascent	Km
Great Borne				98	115	2.0
Red Pike				174	52	2.0

Features visited			
Summit cairn			

Times and Weather			
Departure time			
Arrival time			
Duration			
Weather			
Visibility			

Notes _____

Steeple 819m 2687' NGR NY157117
Landranger 89   Outdoor Leisure 4

Route from				Ascent	Km	Time
Low Gillerthwaite via:						
direct				669	5.0	
Mirk Cove				669	5.5	
Mirklin Cove				669	5.5	

Ridge routes				Descent	Ascent	Km
Scoat Fell				42	20	.75

Features visited			
Summit cairn			

Notes _____

Times and Weather			
Departure time			
Arrival time			
Duration			
Weather			
Visibility			

Whoap 511m 1677' NGR NY099128
Landranger 89   Outdoor Leisure 6

Route from				Ascent	Km	Time
Low Gillerthwaite				361	5.25c	
Near Thwaites c.p. (062130)				251	4.0	

Ridge routes				Descent	Ascent	Km
Caw Fell				199	20	4.5c
Crag Fell				133	120	2.0
Iron Crag				149	20	2.75
Lank Rigg				111	81	1.25

Features visited			
Summit cairn			

Notes _____

Times and Weather			
Departure time			
Arrival time			
Duration			
Weather			
Visibility			

Yewbarrow   628m   1000'   NGR NY173085
Landranger 89 & 90   Outdoor Leisure 6

Route from				Ascent	Km	Time
Overbeck Bridge #				558	4.0	
Wasdale Head #				548	3.0	
Wasdale Head *				548	1.75	

Ridge routes				Descent	Ascent	Km
Red Pike (Wasdale)				381	183	2.5

Features visited			
Summit cairn			
O.S. trig. point			

Times and Weather			
Departure time			
Arrival time			
Duration			
Weather			
Visibility			

Notes _____

_____

_____

_____

_____

_____

_____

_____

_____

Route details: # = via Dore Head, * = via Great Door.

CHAPTER TEN

NORTH WESTERN LAKE DISTRICT

Mountain	Page	Height in Metres	Date first Ascended
Ard Crags	194	581	__:__:__
Barf	194	468	__:__:__
Barrow	195	455	30:08:00
Broom Fell	195	511	__:__:__
Castle Crag	196	299	__:__:__
Cat Bells	196	451	1:9:97
Causey Pike	197	637	__:__:__
Crag Hill (Eel Crag)	197	839	30:08:00
Dale Head	198	753	5:9:97
Grasmoor	199	852	__:__:__
Graystones	199	456	__:__:__
Grisedale Pike	200	791	30:08:00
High Spy	200	653	5:9:97
Hindscarth	201	727	5:9:97
Hobcarton End	201	634	__:__:__
Hopegill Head	202	770	30:08:00
Knott Rigg	202	556	29:08:00
Ladyside Pike	203	703	__:__:__
Ling Fell	203	373	__:__:__
Lord's Seat	204	552	__:__:__
Maiden Moor	204	670	5:9:97
Outerside	205	568	30:08:00
Rannerdale Knotts	205	355	__:__:__
Robinson	206	737	29:08:00
Sail	206	773	30:08:00
Sale Fell	207	359	__:__:__
Sand Hill	207	756	30:08:00
Scar Crags	208	672	__:__:__
Wandope	208	772	__:__:__
Whinlatter	209	525	__:__:__
Whiteless Pike	209	660	__:__:__
Whiteside	210	719	__:__:__

Ard Crags   581m   1906'   NGR NY207198
Landranger 89 & 90   Outdoor Leisure 4

Route from				Ascent	Km	Time
Rigg Beck (229201)				415	2.75c	

Ridge routes				Descent	Ascent	Km
Knott Rigg				51	76	1.25

Features visited				Notes _____
Summit cairn				_____
				_____

Times and Weather				_____
Departure time				_____
Arrival time				_____
Duration				_____
Weather				_____
Visibility				_____

Barf   468m   1535'   NGR NY214268
Landranger 89 & 90   Outdoor Leisure 4

Route from				Ascent	Km	Time
A66 (Hotel) (221264)				368	1.25	

Ridge routes				Descent	Ascent	Km
Lord's Seat				117	33	1.25

Features visited				Notes _____
Summit cairn				_____
The Bishop				_____
The Clerk				_____

Times and Weather				_____
Departure time				_____
Arrival time				_____
Duration				_____
Weather				_____
Visibility				_____

Barrow   455m   1493'   NGR NY226218
Landranger 89 & 90   Outdoor Leisure 4

Route from	30-8-00			Ascent	Km	Time
Braithwaite #	DESCENT			365	2.0	
Braithwaite *				365	2.75	
Stair				355	2.5	

Ridge routes				Descent	Ascent	Km
Outerside	FROM			153	40	1.75

Features visited			
Summit cairn	YES		

Notes 30-8-00
Coffee break en-
route from
Outerside.

Times and Weather			
Departure time	15:56		
Arrival time	16:50		
Duration	54 MINS		
Weather	SUN/GOOD		
Visibility	GOOD		

Route details: # = via
Braithwaite Lodge, * = via High
Coledale and Barrow Door.

Broom Fell   511m   1677'   NGR NY204266   195271
Landranger 89 & 90   Outdoor Leisure 4

Route from				Ascent	Km	Time
Scawgill Bridge c.p.(181256)				286	2.25	
Wythop Mill				411	4.0	

Ridge routes				Descent	Ascent	Km
Graystones				81	136	2.25
Lord's Seat				67	26	1.0

Features visited			
Summit cairn			

Notes

Times and Weather			
Departure time			
Arrival time			
Duration			
Weather			
Visibility			

Castle Crag   299m   981'   NGR NY249159
Landranger 89 & 90   Outdoor Leisure 4

Route from				Ascent	Km	Time
Grange				229	2.0	
Rosthwaite				209	1.5	

Features visited			
Summit cairn			
Summit memorial			
High Hows Caves			
Old quarry workings			

Times and Weather			
Departure time			
Arrival time			
Duration			
Weather			
Visibility			

Notes _____

_____

_____

_____

_____

_____

Castle Crag is clearly not a
mountain, or "top" as popularly
defined, because it is too low.
It is included because it is a
popular climb.It could probably
be classified as a feature of
Low Scawdel or High Spy.

Cat Bells   451m   1480'   NGR NY244198
Landranger 89 & 90   Outdoor Leisure 4

Route from/via	1-9-97			Ascent	Km	Time
Grange	DESCENT			381	3.25	
Hawes End car park/N. ridge	ASCENT			342	1.5	
Little Town				281	1.75	

Ridge routes				Descent	Ascent	Km
Maiden Moor				211	86	2.0

Features visited			
Summit	YES		

Times and Weather			
Departure time	?		
Arrival time	?		
Duration	?		
Weather	SUNNY		
Visibility	V.GOOD		

Notes _____

_____

_____

_____

_____

_____

_____

_____

Causey Pike   637m   2090'   NGR NY219208
Landranger 89 & 90   Outdoor Leisure 4

Route from			Ascent	Km	Time
Stair via Rowling End Farm			537	3.0	
Stair via Stoneycroft			537	2.25	

Ridge routes			Descent	Ascent	Km
Outerside			73	142	2.75
Sail (ignoring Scar Crags)			158	22	2.25
Scar Crags			77	42	1.25

Features visited		
Summit cairn		

Times and Weather		
Departure time		
Arrival time		
Duration		
Weather		
Visibility		

Notes _____
_____
_____
_____
_____

Crag Hill (Eel Crag)   839m   2753'   NGR NY193204
Landranger 89 & 90   Outdoor Leisure 4

Route from	30-8-00		Ascent	Km	Time
Braithwaite			749	5.25	
Lanthwaite c.p. (158207)			689	4.25	

Ridge routes			Descent	Ascent	Km
Grasmoor			147	134	1.75
Grisedale Pike			196	244	2.5
Sail P.206	ONTO		23	89	.65
Sand Hill P.207	FROM		161	244	1.75
Wandope			27	94	1.0

Features visited		
Summit cairn	YES	
O.S. trig. point	YES	

Times and Weather		
Departure time	14:25	
Arrival time	15:05	
Duration	40MINS	
Weather	SUN/CLOUD	
Visibility	FAIR	

Notes _____
_____
_____
_____
_____

Dale Head 753m 2470' NGR NY223153
Landranger 89 & 90   Outdoor Leisure 4

Route from		5.9.97			Ascent	Km	Time
Honister Hause					453	1.75	
Little Town via:							
Dalehead Crags					583	4.75	
Miners Crags					583	5.25	
Rosthwaite					663	3.75	
Seatoller					633	4.25	

Ridge routes					Descent	Ascent	Km
High Spy	P. 200	FROM			148	248	1.75
Hindscarth	P. 201	ONTO			32	58	1.75
Robinson					161	177	2.75

Features visited				
Summit cairn		YES		
Dalehead Tarn		YES		
Launchy Tarn		NO		

Times and Weather				
Departure time		?		
Arrival time		?		
Duration		?		
Weather		CLOUDY		
Visibility		V. GOOD		

Notes _____

_____

_____

_____

_____

_____

_____

_____

_____

_____

_____

_____

_____

_____

_____

_____

_____

Grasmoor 852m 2795' NGR NY175203
Landranger 89 & 90   Outdoor Leisure 4

Route from				Ascent	Km	Time
Lanthwaite car park #				752	2.25	
Lanthwaite car park *				752	5.0	
Rannerdale/Lad Hows 1				742	4.0	
Rannerdale/Red Gill 1				742	1.75	

Ridge routes				Descent	Ascent	Km
Crag Hill				134	147	1.75
Sand Hill				161	257	2.5
Wandope				50	130	2.0

Features visited			
Summit cairn/windshelter			

Times and Weather			
Departure time			
Arrival time			
Duration			
Weather			
Visibility			

Notes _____

_____

_____

_____

_____

_____

Route details: # = via Dove Crag, * = via Gasgale Gill, 1 = from G.R. 162194.

Graystones 456m 1496' NGR NY178264
Landranger 89 & 90   Outdoor Leisure 4

Route from				Ascent	Km	Time
High Lorton				361	2.5	
Scawgill Bridge c. p. (181256)				233	1.5	

Ridge routes				Descent	Ascent	Km
Broom Fell				136	81	2.25

Features visited			
Summit cairn			
Secondary Summit (438m) #			

Times and Weather			
Departure time			
Arrival time			
Duration			
Weather			
Visibility			

Notes _____

_____

_____

_____

_____

_____

_____

Route details: # = Kirk Fell.

Grisedale Pike   791m   2595'   NGR NY189225
Landranger 89 & 90   Outdoor Leisure 4

Route from/via	30-8-00			Ascent	Km	Time
Braithwaite via:						
Coledale Hause				701	6.5	
Sleet How	ASCENT			701	3.5	
Whinlatter Visitor Centre				461	2.5	

Ridge routes				Descent	Ascent	Km
Crag Hill				244	196	2.5
Hobcarton End				15	172	1.0
Hopegill Head	P·202	ONTO		95	116	1.75
Sand Hill		YES		81	116	1.5

Features visited			
Summit cairn	YES		
Lanty Well (spring)	NO		

Notes 30-8-00
Lunch-break
on summit.

Times and Weather			
Departure time B/THWAITE	11:35		
Arrival time	13:20		
Duration	1H 45M		
Weather	SUN GOOD		
Visibility	FAIR		

High Spy   653m   2142'   NGR NY234162
Landranger 89 & 90   Outdoor Leisure 4

Route from	5-9-97			Ascent	Km	Time
Grange				583	3.25	
Little Town/Dalehead Tarn				483	5.25	
Rosthwaite				563	3.5	
Seatoller				533	3.5	

Ridge routes				Descent	Ascent	Km
Dale Head	P.198	ONTO		248	148	1.75
Maiden Moor	P.204	FROM		20	3	2.0

Features visited			
Summit cairn	YES		
North top (634m)	YES		

Notes

Times and Weather			
Departure time	?		
Arrival time	?		
Duration .	?		
Weather	CLOUDY		
Visibility	V.GOOD		

Hindscarth 727m 2385' NGR NY216165
Landranger 89 & 90 Outdoor Leisure 4

Route from/via	S.9.97			Ascent	Km	Time
Gatesgarth/Gatesgarth Beck				607	3.5 - 4.0	
Little Town	DESCENT			557	4.25	

Ridge routes				Descent	Ascent	Km
Dale Head	FROM			58	32	1.75
Robinson				161	151	2.25

Features visited			
Summit cairn	YES		
Summit shelter			

Times and Weather			
Departure time	?		
Arrival time	?		
Duration	?		
Weather	CLOUDY		
Visibility	V. GOOD		

Notes_____

Hobcarton End 634m 2080' NGR NY195235
Landranger 89 & 90 Outdoor Leisure 4

Route from				Ascent	Km	Time
Whinlatter Visitor Centre				304	2.5c	

Ridge routes				Descent	Ascent	Km
Grisedale Pike				172	15	1.0

Features visited			
Summit cairn			

Times and Weather			
Departure time			
Arrival time			
Duration			
Weather			
Visibility			

Notes _____

Hopegill Head   770m   2526'   NGR NY186221
Landranger 89 & 90   Outdoor Leisure 4

Route from	30-8-80			Ascent	Km	Time
Hopebeck via Hope Beck				645	3.5	

Ridge routes				Descent	Ascent	Km
Grisedale Pike P. 200	FROM			116	95	1.75
Ladyside Pike				33	163	.5
Sand Hill P-207	ONTO			21	35	.5
Whiteside	NW			19	70	1.25

Features visited				Notes _____
Summit cairn	YES			

Times and Weather			
Departure time	13:48		
Arrival time	14:16		
Duration	28 MINS		
Weather	SUN/CLOUD		
Visibility	FAIR		

Knott Rigg   556m   1824'   NGR NY197189
Landranger 90   Outdoor Leisure 4

Route from	29-8-00			Ascent	Km	Time
Keskadale Farm	DESCENT			326	1.5	
Newlands Hause	ASCENT			223	1.5	

Ridge routes				Descent	Ascent	Km
Ard Crags				76	51	1.25

Features visited				Notes Came from
Summit stones	YES			Robinson - P.206

Times and Weather			
Departure time	4:35		
Arrival time	5:28		
Duration	53 MINS		
Weather	SUN/CLOUD		
Visibility	V.GOOD		

Ladyside Pike 703m 2307' NGR NY185228
(Lady's Seat) Landranger 89 & 90 Outdoor Leisure 4

Route from				Ascent	Km	Time
High Swinside Farm #				523	2.75	
Hopebeck via Hope Beck				578	3.5	

Ridge routes				Descent	Ascent	Km
Hopegill Head				163	33	.5

Features visited			
Summit cairn			

Times and Weather			
Departure time			
Arrival time			
Duration			
Weather			
Visibility			

Notes_____
_____
_____
_____
_____
_____
_____
_____
_____
_____
_____

Ling Fell 373m 1224' NGR NY179286
Landranger 89 & 90 Outdoor Leisure 4

Route from				Ascent	Km	Time
Wythop Mill				273	1.5	

Features visited			
Summit cairn			
O.S. trig. point			

Times and Weather			
Departure time			
Arrival time			
Duration			
Weather			
Visibility			

Notes _____
_____
_____
_____
_____
_____
_____
_____
_____
_____

Lord's Seat   552m   1811'   NGR NY204266
Landranger 89 & 90   Outdoor Leisure 4

Route from				Ascent	Km	Time
Scawgill Bridge car park				329	2.75	
Whinlatter Visitor Centre				222	3.5c	

Ridge routes				Descent	Ascent	Km
Barf				33	117	1.25
Broom Fell				26	67	1.0

Features visited			
Summit cairn			

Times and Weather			
Departure time			
Arrival time			
Duration			
Weather			
Visibility			

Notes _____
_____
_____
_____
_____
_____
_____
_____
_____
_____

Maiden Moor   ~576m~ 670m   2198'   NGR NY237182
Landranger 90   Outdoor Leisure 4

Route from	5-9-97			Ascent	Km	Time
Grange via Manesty				600	4.0	
Grange via Nitting Haws				600	4.0	
Little Town	ASCENT			500	2.25	

Ridge routes				Descent	Ascent	Km
Cat Bells				86	211	2.0
High Spy	P.200	ONTO		3	20	2.0

Features visited			
Summit cairn	YES		

Times and Weather			
Departure time	?		
Arrival time	?		
Duration	?		
Weather	CLOUDY		
Visibility	V.GOOD		

Notes _____
_____
_____
_____
_____
_____
_____
_____
_____

Outerside   568m   1864'   NGR NY211214
Landranger 90   Outdoor Leisure 4

Route from	30-8-00			Ascent	Km	Time
Braithwaite via:						
Barrow Door				478	3.3	
Low Moss				478	3.15	
Stile End				478	3.25	
Stair				468	2.75	

Ridge routes				Descent	Ascent	Km
Barrow	P.195	ONTO		40	153	1.75
Causey Pike #				142	73	2.75
Sail	P-206	FROM		278	73	2.0
Scar Crags				177	73	1.5

Features visited			
Summit cairn	YES		

Times and Weather			
Departure time	15:25		
Arrival time	15:55		
Duration	30MINS		
Weather	SUN/COLD		
Visibility	GOOD		

Notes _____

_____

_____

_____

_____

_____

_____

Route details: # = ignoring Scar Crags.

Rannerdale Knotts   355m   1165'   NGR NY167182
Landranger 89   Outdoor Leisure 4

Route from				Ascent	Km	Time
Buttermere				243	2.5	
Car park @ 162182				235	.75	

Ridge routes				Descent	Ascent	Km
Whiteless Pike				360	55	2.5c

Features visited			
Summit cairn			

Times and Weather			
Departure time			
Arrival time			
Duration			
Weather			
Visibility			

Notes _____

_____

_____

_____

_____

_____

_____

_____

Robinson   737m   2418'   NGR NY202169
Landranger 89   Outdoor Leisure 4

Route from	29.8.00			Ascent	Km	Time
Buttermere				625	3.0	
Gatesgarth #				617	4.5c	
Little Town 1				667	4.75	
Little Town 2				667	4.5	
Newlands Hause	DESCENT			404	2.0	
B5289 @ Dalegarth				597	2.0	
KESKADALE / HIGH SNAB	ASCENT					

Ridge routes → H. SNAB BANK	YES			Descent	Ascent	Km
Dale Head				177	161	2.75
Hindscarth				151	161	2.25

Features visited			
Summit cairn/shelter	YES		

Notes Went on to
Knott Rigg – P.202

Times and Weather			
Departure time (KESKADALE)	13:18		
Arrival time	15:07		
Duration	1HR 49m		
Weather	SUN / CLOUD		
Visibility	V. GOOD		

Route details: # = via
Gatesgarthdale Beck and
Litterdale Edge, 1 = via High
Snab Bank, 2 = via Scope
Bank.

Sail   773m   2536'   NGR NY198203
Landranger 89 & 90   Outdoor Leisure 4

Route from	30-8-00			Ascent	Km	Time
Braithwaite #				683	5.0	
Stair #				663	4.5	

Ridge routes				Descent	Ascent	Km
Causey Pike *				22	158	2.25
Crag Hill P. 197	FROM			89	23	.65
Outerside P. 205	ONTO			73	278	2.0
Scar Crags				57	158	1.25

Features visited			
Summit cairn	YES		

Notes _____

Times and Weather			
Departure time	15:06		
Arrival time	15:24		
Duration	18MINS		
Weather	SUN / CLOUD		
Visibility	GOOD		

Route details: # = passing
south of Outerside summit,
* = ignoring Scar Crags.

Sale Fell   359m   1178'   NGR NY194296
Landranger 89 & 90 Outdoor Leisure 4

Route from				Ascent	Km	Time
Wythop Mill				199	2.0c	

Features visited				Notes
Summit cairn				
Walton Memorial				

Times and Weather			
Departure time			
Arrival time			
Duration			
Weather			
Visibility			

Sand Hill   756m   2480'   NGR NY187219
Landranger 89 & 90   Outdoor Leisure 4

Route from	30-8-00			Ascent	Km	Time
Braithwaite				666	5.75	
Lanthwaite Green c. p. #				606	4.0	

Ridge routes				Descent	Ascent	Km
Crag Hill P 197	ONTO			244	161	1.75
Grasmoor				257	161	2.5
Grisedale Pike				116	81	1.5
Hopegill Head P. 202	FROM			35	21	.5

Features visited				Notes
Summit cairn	YES			

Times and Weather			
Departure time	14:17		
Arrival time	14:25		
Duration	8 MINS		
Weather	SUN/CLOUD		
Visibility	FAIR		

Route details: # = from G.R.
158207.

Scar Crags   672m   2205'   NGR NY208206
Landranger 89 & 90   Outdoor Leisure 4

Route from				Ascent	Km	Time
Braithwaite				582	4.0 - 4.5	

Ridge routes				Descent	Ascent	Km
Causey Pike				42	77	1.25
Outerside				77	177	1.5
Sail				158	57	1.25

Features visited			
Summit cairn			

Times and Weather			
Departure time			
Arrival time			
Duration			
Weather			
Visibility			

Notes _____
_____
_____
_____
_____
_____
_____
_____
_____

Wandope   772m   2533'   NGR NY188197
Landranger 89 & 90   Outdoor Leisure 4

Route from				Ascent	Km	Time
Buttermere #				660	5.0	
Buttermere *				660	4.5	

Ridge routes				Descent	Ascent	Km
Crag Hill				94	27	1.0
Grasmoor				130	50	2.0
Whiteless Pike				35	147	1.25

Features visited			
Summit cairn			

Times and Weather			
Departure time			
Arrival time			
Duration			
Weather			
Visibility			

Notes _____
_____
_____
_____
_____
_____
_____

Route details: # = via
Addacomb Hole, * = via Third
Gill.

Whinlatter 525m 1722' NGR NY198249
Landranger 89 & 90 Outdoor Leisure 4

Route from				Ascent	Km	Time
Whinlatter Visitor Centre				195	1.25	

Features visited				Notes _____
Summit cairn				
West top (Brown How) (517m)				

Times and Weather			
Departure time			
Arrival time			
Duration			
Weather			
Visibility			

Whiteless Pike 660m 2165' NGR NY180190
Landranger 89 & 90 Outdoor Leisure 90

Route from				Ascent	Km	Time
Buttermere				548	2.25	

Ridge routes				Descent	Ascent	Km
Rannerdale Knotts				55	360	2.5
Wandope				147	35	1.25

Features visited				Notes _____
Summit cairn				

Times and Weather			
Departure time			
Arrival time			
Duration			
Weather			
Visibility			

Whiteside   719m   2359'   NGR NY175221

Landranger 89 & 90   Outdoor Leisure 4

Route from				Ascent	Km	Time
Brackenthwaite				569c	2.0c	
Hopebeck via Cold Gill				594	3.75	
Lanthwaite Green c.p. (158207)				569	2.25	

Ridge routes				Descent	Ascent	Km
Hopegill Head				70	19	1.25

Features visited			
Summit cairn			
West top (707m)			
Whin Ben (413m)			

Times and Weather			
Departure time			
Arrival time			
Duration			
Weather			
Visibility			

Notes _____
_____
_____
_____
_____
_____
_____
_____
_____
_____
_____

CHAPTER ELEVEN

CENTRAL LAKE DISTRICT

Mountain	Page	Height in Metres	Date first Ascended
Armboth Fell	212	479	__:__:__
Bleaberry Fell	212	590	MAY :92
Blea Rigg	213	541	__:__:__
Calf Crag	213	537	__:__:__
Codale Head	214	730	__:__:__
Gibson Knott	214	410	__:__:__
Grange Fell	215	415	__:__:__
Great Crag	215	440	__:__:__
Harrison Stickle	216	736	1:9:99
Helm Crag	217	405	9:5:05
High Raise	218	762	__:__:__
High Rigg	218	350	__:__:__
High Seat	219	608	MAY :92
High Tove	219	515	3:9:99
Loft Crag	220	670	__:__:__
Loughrigg Fell	220	335	2:9:96
Low Saddle	221	656	__:__:__
Pavey Ark	221	700	1:9:99
Pike of Stickle	222	709	1:9:99
Raven Crag	222	461	__:__:__
Sergeant Man	223	730	__:__:__
Silver How	223	395	__:__:__
Steel Fell	224	553	__:__:__
Tarn Crag	224	550	__:__:__
Thurnacar Knott	225	723	__:__:__
Ullscarf	226	726	__:__:__
Walla Crag	226	379	__:__:__

Armboth Fell   479m   1572'   NGR NY298158
Landranger 90   Outdoor Leisure 4

Route from				Ascent	Km	Time
Armboth (305172)				290	2.0	
Dobgill Bridge (316170)				290	4.0	
Thirlmere (309158) #				290	1.5	

Ridge routes				Descent	Ascent	Km
High Tove				36	nil	1.5
Ullscarf				247	24	4.5

Features visited			
Summit cairn			
Fisher Crag			
Launchy Tarn			
Harrop Tarn			

Times and Weather			
Departure time			
Arrival time			
Duration			
Weather			
Visibility			

Notes _____
_____
_____
_____
_____
_____
_____
_____
_____
_____
_____

Route details: # = via
Launchy Gill.

Bleaberry Fell   590m   1936'   NGR NY285195
Landranger 89 & 90   Outdoor Leisure 4

Route from	MAY 92			Ascent	Km	Time
Ashness Bridge				435	1.75c	
Borrowdale Road				513	3.0	
Keswick				490c	4.75-5.5	

Ridge routes				Descent	Ascent	Km
High Seat	P.219	ONTO		58	40	1.5
Walla Crag	P.226	FROM		nil	211	2.25

Features visited	YES		
Summit cairn			

Times and Weather			
Departure time	?		
Arrival time	?		
Duration	?		
Weather	D.C.W		
Visibility	V.GOOD		

Notes _____
_____
_____
_____
_____
_____
_____

Blea Rigg   541m   1775'   NGR NY299079
Landranger 89 & 90   Outdoor Leisure 4, 6 & 7

Route from/via	10.9.07			Ascent	Km	Time
Grasmere via Belles Knott				481	6.0	
Grasmere via Blea Crag	ASCENT			481	5.0	
New Dungeon Ghyll Hotel #				451	2.5	
New Dungeon Ghyll Hotel *				451	2.0	
PAVEY ARK	ONTO					

Ridge routes				Descent	Ascent	Km
Sergeant Man				189	nil	1.75
Silver How				20	166	3.5

Features visited			
Summit cairn			
Easedale Tarn			
Stickle Tarn			

Times and Weather			
Departure time			
Arrival time			
Duration			
Weather			
Visibility			

Notes _____
_____
_____
_____
_____
_____
_____
_____
_____

Route details: # = via Tarn
Crag, * = via Whitegill Crag.

Calf Crag   537m   1762'   NGR NY302104
Landranger 90   Outdoor Leisure 6 & 7

Route from				Ascent	Km	Time
Grasmere via Far Easedale				577	6.0	
Grasmere via Greenburn				577	5.5	

Ridge routes				Descent	Ascent	Km
Codale Head				245	52	2.0
Gibson Knott				nil	120	2.2
Steel Fell				78	62	2.5

Features visited			
Summit cairn			

Times and Weather			
Departure time			
Arrival time			
Duration			
Weather			
Visibility			

Notes _____
_____
_____
_____

Ordnance Survey maps quote
three different heights for this
fell: Landranger 90 = 537m,
Outdoor Leisure 6 = 520m and
Outdoor Leisure 7 = 530m.

Codale Head   730m   2395'   NGR NY289091
Landranger 89 & 90   Outdoor Leisure 4 & 6

Route from				Ascent	Km	Time
Grasmere via Far Easedale				670	6.5	

Ridge routes				Descent	Ascent	Km
Calf Crag				52	245	2.0
High Raise				32	nil	1.0
Sergeant Man				5	5	.5
Steel Fell				68	245	4.0

Features visited				Notes
Summit cairn				

Times and Weather			
Departure time			
Arrival time			
Duration			
Weather			
Visibility			

Gibson Knott   410m   1345'   NGR NY321098
Landranger 90   Outdoor Leisure 4, 6 & 7

Route from				Ascent	Km	Time
Grasmere #				350	3.5	
Grasmere *				350	3.5	

Ridge routes				Descent	Ascent	Km
Calf Crag				120	nil	2.2
Helm Crag				55	65	.75

Features visited				Notes
Summit cairn				

Times and Weather			
Departure time			
Arrival time			
Duration			
Weather			
Visibility			

Route details: # = via
Greenburn and Bracken
Hause,* = via Easedale and
Bracken Hause.

Grange Fell   415m   1362' NGR NY264163
Landranger 89 & 90   Outdoor Leisure 4

Route from				Ascent	Km	Time
Grange				345	1.75 - 2.5	
Rosthwaite				325	2.0 - 2.75	
Watendlath				145	1.5 - 2.25	

Features visited				Notes _____
Summits of :				_____
Brund Fell				_____
Ether Knott				_____
Jopplety How				_____
Kings How (392m)				_____
				_____

Times and Weather				_____
Departure time				_____
Arrival time				_____
Duration				_____
Weather				_____
Visibility				_____

Great Crag   440m   1444' NGR NY264148
Landranger 89 & 90   Outdoor Leisure 4

Route from				Ascent	Km	Time
Stonethwaite				340	2.0	
Watendlath				170	2.0	

Ridge routes				Descent	Ascent	Km
Low Saddle				296	80	2.5
Ullscarf #				366	80	3.5

Features visited				Notes _____
Summit cairn				_____
Dock Tarn				_____
				_____

Times and Weather				_____
Departure time				_____
Arrival time				_____
Duration				_____
Weather				Route details: # = avoiding
Visibility				Low Saddle.

Harrison Stickle   736m   2415'   NGR NY282074
Landranger 89 & 90   Outdoor Leisure 6

Route from	1-9-99	10-9-07	Ascent	Km	Time
New Dungeon Ghyll Hotel via:					
Dungeon Ghyll Ravines			646	2.25	
Stickle Tarn			646	2.0	
Thorn Crag			646	1.85	
Old Dungeon Ghyll Hotel via:					
Dungeon Ghyll Ravines			636	2.0	
Stickle Tarn			636	2.75	
Thorn Crag			636	2.5	
MICKLEDON					

Ridge routes			Descent	Ascent	Km
Loft Crag			60	126	.5
Pavey Ark P.221	ONTO	FROM	nil	36	.85
Pike of Stickle P.222	FROM		84	111	.75
Rossett Pike			166	251	4.5
Thurnacar Knott P.225	NO	ONTO	28	5	.75

Features visited				
Summit cairn	YES	YES		
South cairn	YES	NO		
Dungeon Ghyll Force	NO	NO		
Stickle Tarn	YES	NO		

Times and Weather				
Departure time	?			
Arrival time	?			
Duration	?			
Weather	DRY WINDY *	DRY WINDY		
Visibility	GOOD *	V. GOOD		

Notes * The poor weather & visibility referred to on P. 222 had improved considerably by the time we reached Harrison Stickle.

Helm Crag   405m   1329'   NGR NY326093
Landranger 90   Outdoor Leisure 4, 6 & 7

Route from	9-5-05			Ascent	Km	Time
Grasmere via White Crag	DESCENT			345	2.75	?
Town Head (333099) #	ASCENT			270	1.5	?

Ridge routes				Descent	Ascent	Km
Gibson Knott	NO			65	55	.75

Features visited			
Summit cairn	YES		
Lion and Lamb	YES		

Times and Weather			
Departure time	?		
Arrival time	?		
Duration	?		
Weather ✳	VARIABLE		
Visibility	EXCELLENT		

Notes ✳ The weather alternated between hails and warm sunshine !! A great view from the top — nice pit-stop in better weather.

Route details: # = via Bracken Hause.

High Raise   762m   2500'   NGR NY281095
Landranger 89   Outdoor Leisure 4, 6 & 7

Route from/via	10-9-07			Ascent	Km	Time
Grasmere/Far Easedale #				702	7.5	
New Dungeon Ghyll Hotel *				672	4.25c	
Stonethwaite				662	5.5	
Wythburn				572	5.5	

Ridge routes				Descent	Ascent	Km
Codale Head				nil	32	1.0
Pavey Ark				15	77	2.0
Rossett Pike				166	277	4.0
Sergeant Man	P.223	ONTO		nil	32	.75
Thurnacar Knott	P.225	FROM		38	77	1.5
Ullscarf				121	157	3.0

Features visited				Notes _____
Summit (High White Stones) shelter	YES			_____
O.S. trig. point	YES			_____
Eagle Crag (510m) (276121)	NO			_____
Sergeant's Crag (571m) 1	NO			_____
Low White Stones (730m) 2	NO			_____

Times and Weather				_____
Departure time				_____
Arrival time				_____
Duration				Route details: # = via Far
Weather	DRY, WINDY			Easedale and Greenup Edge,*
Visibility	V.GOOD			= via Bright Beck, 1 = @ G.R.

Route details: # = via Far Easedale and Greenup Edge,* = via Bright Beck, 1 = @ G.R. 274114, 2 = @ G. R. 282101.

High Rigg   350m   1148'   NGR NY220307 213
Landranger 89 & 90   Outdoor Leisure 4 & 5

Route from				Ascent	Km	Time
St John's in the Vale church				140	1.25	

Features visited				Notes _____
Summit cairn				_____
				_____

Times and Weather				_____
Departure time				_____
Arrival time				_____
Duration				_____
Weather				_____
Visibility				_____

High Seat   608m   1995'   NGR NY288180
Landranger 89 & 90   Outdoor Leisure 4

Route from	MAY 92			Ascent	Km	Time
Armboth (direct)				469	2.5	
Ashness Bridge	DESCENT			453	2.5	
Watendlath Road @ 271178				375	1.5	
Watendlath c. p. via above				338	3.25	
A591 (297214)				438	4.0	

Ridge routes				Descent	Ascent	Km
Bleaberry Fell P212	FROM			40	58	1.5
High Tove				15	108	1.75

Features visited				Notes
Summit cairn	YES			
O.S. trig. point	YES			
Litt's Memorial	NO			
Pouterhow Pike	NO			

Times and Weather			
Departure time			
Arrival time			
Duration			
Weather			
Visibility			

High Tove   515m   1690'   NGR NY289165
Landranger 89 & 90   Outdoor Leisure 4

Route from	3-9-99			Ascent	Km	Time
Armboth	ASCENT			326	1.75	
Watendlath				245	1.2 - 1.4	

Ridge routes				Descent	Ascent	Km
Armboth Fell	NO			nil	36	1.5
High Seat	NO			108	15	1.75
Ullscarf	NO			251	40	5.0

Features visited				Notes
Summit cairn	YES			

Times and Weather			
Departure time	?		
Arrival time	?		
Duration	?		
Weather	DRY SUNNY		
Visibility	V. GOOD		

Loft Crag   670m   2198'   NGR NY277071
Landranger 89 & 90   Outdoor Leisure 4

Route from				Ascent	Km	Time
New Dungeon Ghyll Hotel				580	2.0	
Old Dungeon Ghyll Hotel				570	1.25	

Ridge routes				Descent	Ascent	Km
Harrison Stickle				126	60	.5
Pike of Stickle				49	60	.5
Rossett Pike				166	185	4.5

Features visited				Notes _____
Summit cairn				
Gimmer Crag				
Thorn Crag				

Times and Weather			
Departure time			
Arrival time			
Duration			
Weather			
Visibility			

Loughrigg Fell   335m   1099'   NGR NY347051
Landranger 90   Outdoor Leisure 7

Route from	29-96			Ascent	Km	Time
Ambleside	ASCENT			245	3.5	
Clappersgate				285	3.0	
Grasmere	DESCENT			275	3.25	
Skelwith Bridge				295	2.5	
White Moss car park				265	2.0	

Ridge routes				Descent	Ascent	Km
Silver How	NO			232	172	3.5

Features visited				Notes _____
O.S. trig. point				
Ivy Crag				
Loughrigg Force				
Big Cave (above quarry)				

Times and Weather			
Departure time			
Arrival time			
Duration			
Weather	HOT SUN		
Visibility	V.GOOD		

Low Saddle 656m 2152' NGR NY288133
Landranger 89 & 90 Outdoor Leisure 4

Route from				Ascent	Km	Time
Watendlath				386	3.5	

Ridge routes				Descent	Ascent	Km
Great Crag				80	296	2.5
Ullscarf				70	nil	1.1

Features visited			
Summit cairn			

Times and Weather			
Departure time			
Arrival time			
Duration			
Weather			
Visibility			

Notes _____
_____
_____
_____
_____
_____
_____
_____
_____
_____
_____

Pavey Ark 700m 2297' NGR NY285079
Landranger 89 & 90 Outdoor Leisure 6

Route from	1-9-99	10-9-07		Ascent	Km	Time
New Dungeon Ghyll Hotel via:						
Bright Beck	DESCENT			610	3.0	?
Easy Gully				610	2.25	
Path to Harrison Stickle				610	2.25	
Jack's Rake				610	2.25	
North Gully				610	2.5	

213 BLEA RIGG (Nth Gully?) — FROM

Ridge routes				Descent	Ascent	Km
Harrison Stickle P. 216	FROM	ONTO		36	nil	.85
High Raise				77	15	2.0
Thurnacar Knott				33	10	.5

Features visited			
Summit cairn	YES	NO	
Stickle Tarn	YES	NO	

Times and Weather			
Departure time			
Arrival time			
Duration			
Weather	DRY WINDY	DRY WINDY	
Visibility	GOOD	V. GOOD	

Notes _____
_____
_____
_____
_____
_____
_____
_____
_____
_____

Pike of Stickle   709m   2326'   NGR NY274074
Landranger 89 & 90   Outdoor Leisure 6

Route from	1-9-99			Ascent	Km	Time
Old Dungeon Ghyll Hotel via:						
Grave Gill				609	2.25	
Scree Gully				609	2.25	
Stake Pass				609	6.25	
Troughton Beck	ASCENT			609	4.0	

Ridge routes				Descent	Ascent	Km
Harrison Stickle P. 216	ONTO			111	84	.75
Loft Crag				60	49	.5
Rossett Pike				166	224	4.0

Features visited			
Summit cairn	YES		
South Scree Cave	NO		
Martcragmoor cairn (547m)	NO		

Times and Weather			
Departure time	?		
Arrival time	?		
Duration	?		
Weather	POOR		
Visibility	V. POOR		

Notes _____

Raven Crag   461m   1513'   NGR NY303188
Landranger 90   Outdoor Leisure 4

Route from				Ascent	Km	Time
Thirlmere Dam				281	1.25	

Features visited			
Summit cairn			
Castle Crag Fort			

Times and Weather			
Departure time			
Arrival time			
Duration			
Weather			
Visibility			

Notes _____

Sergeant Man 730m 2395' NGR NY286089
Landranger 89 & 90   Outdoor Leisure 6 & 7

Route from/via	10-9-07			Ascent	Km	Time
Grasmere/Easedale Tarn	DESCENT			670	5.75	
Grasmere/Codale Tarn				670	5.5	
New Dungeon Ghyll Hotel				640	3.25	

Ridge routes				Descent	Ascent	Km
Blea Rigg				nil	189	1.75
Codale Head				5	45	.5
High Raise	P218	FROM		32	nil	.75
Tarn Crag #				10	190	1.5
Thurnacar Knott				48	55	1.5

Features visited			
Summit cairn	YES		
Codale Tarn	NO		
Easedale Tarn	YES		
Stickle Tarn	NO		

Times and Weather			
Departure time			
Arrival time			
Duration			
Weather	DRY, WINDY		
Visibility	V. GOOD		

Notes _____

Route details: # = ignoring
Codale Head.

Silver How 395m 1296' NGR NY325066
Landranger 90   Outdoor Leisure 6 & 7

Route from				Ascent	Km	Time
Chapel Stile				310	1.5 - 2.0	
Elterwater				325	2.5	
Grasmere				335	2.0	

Ridge routes				Descent	Ascent	Km
Blea Rigg				166	20	3.5

Features visited			
Summit cairn			
Lang How (414m)			

Times and Weather			
Departure time			
Arrival time			
Duration			
Weather			
Visibility			

Notes _____

Steel Fell   553m   1814'   NGR NY319111
Landranger 90   Outdoor Leisure 4, 5 & 7

Route from/via				Ascent	Km	Time
Dunmail Raise				313	1.2	
Grasmere/Cotra Breast				493	4.25	
Wythburn				363	2.0	

Ridge routes				Descent	Ascent	Km
Calf Crag				62	78	2.5
Codale Head				245	68	4.0

Features visited				Notes
Summit cairn (Dead Pike)				

Times and Weather			
Departure time			
Arrival time			
Duration			
Weather			
Visibility			

Tarn Crag   550m   1805'   NGR NY303093
Landranger 90   Outdoor Leisure 4, 5 & 7

Route from/via				Ascent	Km	Time
Grasmere/Easedale Tarn				490	4.25	
Grasmere via East ridge				490	4.25	
Grasmere/Stythwaite Steps #				490	4.5	

Ridge routes				Descent	Ascent	Km
Sergeant Man				190	10	1.5

Features visited				Notes
Summit cairn				
Easedale Tarn				

Times and Weather			
Departure time			
Arrival time			
Duration			
Weather			
Visibility			

Route details: # = via also the
East ridge.

Thurnacar Knott   723m   2372' NGR NY279080
Landranger 89 & 90   Outdoor Leisure 6

Route from	10.9.07			Ascent	Km	Time
New Dungeon Ghyll Hotel				633	7.7 #	

Ridge routes				Descent	Ascent	Km
Harrison Stickle	FROM			5	28	.75
High Raise P-218	ONTO			77	38	1.5
Pavey Ark				10	33	.5
Rossett Pike				166	238	4.25
Sergeant Man				55	48	1.5

Features visited			
Summit cairns	YES		

Times and Weather			
Departure time			
Arrival time			
Duration			
Weather	DRY WINDY		
Visibility	V.GOOD		

Notes

It is unlikely that ascent would be made without first visiting the Landgale Pikes. A direct ascent via Stake Pass is possible and the details quoted are for this route.

Ullscarf   726m   2382'   NGR NY291122
Landranger 89 & 90   Outdoor Leisure 4 & 7

Route from/via				Ascent	Km	Time
Dobgill Bridge/Harrop Tarn				537	4.5	
Grasmere/Greenup Edge				666	8.0	
Stonethwaite/Greenup Edge				626	6.0	
Watendlath				456	5.5	
Wythburn direct				536	3.75	
Wythburn via Wyth Burn				536	6.25	

Ridge routes				Descent	Ascent	Km
Armboth Fell				24	247	4.5
Great Crag				80	366	3.5
High Raise				157	121	3.0
High Tove				40	251	5.0

Features visited				Notes _____
Summit cairn				_____
Coldbarrow Fell (656m)				_____
Binka Stone				_____
Harrop Tarn				_____

Times and Weather				_____
Departure time				_____
Arrival time				_____
Duration				_____
Weather				_____
Visibility				_____

Walla Crag   379m   1244'   NGR NY277213
Landranger 89 & 90   Outdoor Leisure 4

Route from	*MAY 92*			Ascent	Km	Time
Borrowdale Road				299c	1.5c	
Keswick				289c	3.5c	
Castlerigg Campsite	*ASCENT*					

Ridge routes				Descent	Ascent	Km
Bleaberry Fell *P212 ONTO*				211	nil	2.25

Features visited				Notes _____
Summit cairn				_____
				_____

Times and Weather				_____
Departure time				_____
Arrival time				_____
Duration				_____
Weather				_____
Visibility				_____

Appendix One

MOUNTAINS IN DESCENDING HEIGHT ORDER

Mountain	Height in metres
Scafell Pike	978
Scafell	964
Helvellyn	950
Ill Crag	935
Broad Crag	934
Skiddaw	931
Helvellyn Lower Man	925
Great End	910
Bowfell	902
Great Gable	899
Cross Fell	893
Pillar	892
Nethermost Pike	891
Catstye Cam	890
Esk Pike	885
Raise	883
Fairfield	873
Blencathra	868
Skiddaw Little Man	865
White Side	863
Crinkle Crags	859
Dollywaggon Pike	858
Great Dodd	857
Grasmoor	852
Great Dun Fell	848
Stybarrow Dodd	843
Little Dun Fell	842
Saint Sunday Crag	841
Scoat Fell	841
Crag Hill (Eel Crag) (N. W. Lake District)	839
Black Crag	828
High Street	828
Red Pike Wasdale	826
Hart Crag	822
Steeple	819
The Cheviot	815
High Stile	807
The Old Man of Coniston	803
High Raise (F. E. Lake District)	802
Kirk Fell	802

Mountain	Height in metres
Swirl How	802
Green Gable	801
Lingmell	800
Haycock	797
Brim Fell	796
Green Side	795
Knock Fell	794
Dove Crag	792
Rampsgill Head	792
Grisedale Pike	791
Watson's Dodd	789
Mickle Fell	788
Allen Crags	785
Great Carrs	785
Thornthwaite Crag	784
Glaramara	783
Kidsty Pike	780
Dow Crag	778
Harter Fell (F. E. Lake District)	778
Cairn Hill	776
Red Screes	776
Sail	773
Wandope	772
Grey Friar	770
Hopegill Head	770
Meldon Hill	767
Great Rigg (inc. Stone Arthur)	766
Stoney Cove Pike	763
Weatherlam	763
High Raise (C. Lake District)	762
Slight Side	762
Mardale Ill Bell	760
Ill Bell	757
Hart Side	756
Sand Hill	756
Red Pike Buttermere	755
Dale Head	753
Little Fell (Pennines)	748
Burnhope Seat	746
Carl Side	746
Black Sails	745
Buck Pike	744
High Crag	744
Hangingstone Hill	743
Little Stand	740
The Knott	739
Robinson	737
Harrison Stickle	736
Seat Sandal	736
Whernside	736

Mountain	Height in metres
Long Side	734
Codale Head	730
Kentmere Pike	730
Sergeant Man	730
Hindscarth	727
Auchope Cairn	726
Clough Head	726
Ullscarf	726
Ingleborough	723
Thurnacar Knott	723
Froswick	720
Whiteside	719
Birkhouse Moor	718
Harwood Common	718
Great Shunner Fell	716
Brandreth	715
Lonscale Fell	715
Hedgehope Hill	714
Branstree	713
Dead Stones	710
Knott	710
High Seat (Yorkshire Dales)	709
Melmerby Fell	709
Pike of Stickle	709
Great Stony Hill	708
Wild Boar Fell	708
Yoke	706
Pike of Blisco	705
Great Whernside	704
Chapfell Top	703
Ladyside Pike	703
Bowscale Fell	702
Buckden Pike	702
Cold Pike	701
Pavey Ark	700
Backstone Edge	699
Gray Crag	699
Grey Knotts	697
Fendrith Hill	696
Rest Dodd	696
Archy Styrigg	695
Pen-y-ghent	694
Scaud Hill	694
Seatallan	693
Caw Fell	690
Great Calva	690
Hugh Seat	688
Great Coum	687
Round Hill	686
Bannerdale Crags	683

Mountain	Height in metres
Brown Pike	682
Crag Hill (Yorkshire Dales)	682
Swarth Fell	681
Plover Hill	680
Ullock Pike	680
Baugh Fell	678
The Calf	676
Knoutberry Haw	676
Lovely Seat	675
Murton Fell	675
Sheffield Pike	675
Westernhope Moor	675
Calders	674
Bakestall	673
Killhope Law	673
Bram Rigg Top	672
Great Knoutberry Hill	672
Rogan's Seat	672
Scar Crags	672
Loadpot Hill	671
Loft Crag	670
Maiden Moor	670
Wether Hill	670
Dodd Fell Hill	668
Fountains Fell	668
Knoutberry Hill	668
Water Crag	668
Little Fell (Yorkshire Dales)	667
Sails	666
Sale How	666
Black Fell (Pennines)	664
Tarn Crag (F. E. Lake District)	664
Nine Standards Rigg	662
Carrock Fell	660
Whiteless Pike	660
High Pike (N. Lake District)	658
Long Man Hill	658
Place Fell	657
Grey Nag	656
High Pike (E. Lake District)	656
Low Saddle	656
Selside Pike	655
Middle Dodd	654
Harter Fell (S. Lake District)	653
High Spy	653
Outberry Plain	653
Comb Fell	652
Great Sca Fell	651
Rossett Pike	651
Three Pikes	651
Simon Fell	650

Mountain	Height in metres
Viewing Hill	649
Fleetwith Pike	648
Base Brown	646
Black Hill (Pennines)	645
Yockenthwaite Moor	643
High Pike Hill	642
Little Calva	642
Fell Head	640
Iron Crag	640
Yarlside	639
Grey Crag	638
Causey Pike	637
Little Hart Crag	637
Harrop Pike	637
Tom Smith's Stone	637
Kinder Scout	636
Fiend's Fell	634
Hobcarton End	634
Bleaklow Head	633
Mungrisdale Common	633
Starling Dodd	633
Seathwaite Fell	632
Green Hill	628
Rough Crag	628
Yewbarrow	628
Gragareth	627
Darnbrook Fell	624
Randygill Top	624
Bush Howe	623
Birks	622
Cold Fell	621
Higher Shelf Stones	621
High Willhays	621
Walna Scar	621
Bellbeaver Rigg	620
Bink Moss	619
Windy Gyle	619
Yes Tor	619
Hartsop Dodd	618
Tor Mere Top	617
Cushat Law	616
Great Borne	616
Great Lingy Hill	616
The Dodd	614
Drumaldrace	614
Flinty Fell	614
Burtree Fell	612
Heron Pike	612
Middlehope Moor	612
Rosthwaite Fell	612
Birks Fell	610

Mountain	Height in metres
Bloodybush Edge	610
Bullman Hills	610
White Maiden	610
Illgill Head	609
Thack Moor	609
High Seat (C. Lake District)	608
Arant Haw	606
The Schil	605
Peel Fell	602
Watch Hill	602
Haystacks	597
Croglin Fell	591
Bleaberry Fell	590
Shipman Knotts	587
Brae Fell	585
Black Hill (Peak District)	582
Middle Fell	582
Ard Crags	581
The Nab	576
Wansfell Pike	576
Blake Fell	573
Whitfell	573
Hartsop-above-How	570
Brown Knoll	569
Deadwater Fell	569
Outerside	568
Angletarn Pikes	567
The Curr	564
Beefstand Hill	561
Brock Crags	561
Mid Fell	561
Knott Rigg	556
Rise Hill	556
Steel Fell	553
Lord's Seat (N. W. Lake District)	552
Mozie Law	552
Carlin Tooth	551
Lord's Seat (Peak District)	550
Tarn Crag (C. Lake District)	550
Black Hag	549
Hard Knott	549
Margery Hill	546
Hartshorn Pike	545
Mill Hill	544
Blea Rigg	541
Lank Rigg	541
Meal Fell	540
Back Tor	538
Calf Crag	537
Great Mell Fell	537

Mountain	Height in metres
Whin Rigg	535
Arthur's Pike	532
Bonscale Pike	530
Gavel Fell	526
Great Cockup	526
Whinlatter	525
Crag Fell	523
Souther Fell	522
High Hartsop Dodd	519
Mam Tor	517
Sallows	516
High Tove	515
Mellbreak	512
Broom Fell	511
Lamb Hill	511
Whoap	511
Beda Fell	509
Hen Comb	509
Low Pike	508
Little Mell Fell	505
Dodd	502
Green Crag	488
Grike	488
Wansfell	487
Sour Howes	483
Longlands Fell	482
Gowbarrow Fell	481
Armboth Fell	479
Burnbank Fell	475
Lingmoor Fell	469
Barf	468
Raven Crag	461
High Neb	458
Graystones	456
Barrow	455
Cat Bells	451
Binsey	447
Nab Scar	445
Glenridding Dodd	442
Great Crag	440
Arnison Crag	433
Steel Knotts	432
Low Fell	423
Fellbarrow	416
Grange Fell	415
Gibson Knott	410
Helm Crag	405
Buckbarrow	400
Silver How	395

Mountain	Height in metres
Hallin Fell	388
Walla Crag	379
Ling Fell	373
Latrigg	367
Troutbeck Tongue	364
Sale Fell	359
Rannerdale Knotts	355
High Rigg	350
Loughrigg Fell	335
Black Fell (S. Lake District)	322
Holme Fell	317
Castle Crag	299

Appendix Two

MAPS REQUIRED BY AREA

THE CHEVIOTS and KIELDER
Ordnance Survey Explorer, 1:25 000

Sheet Number	Area
1	Kielder Water

Ordnance Survey Landranger, 1:50 000

Sheet Number	Area
74	Kelso
75	Berwick-upon-Tweed and surrounding area
80	Cheviot Hills and Kielder Forest area

PENNINES
Ordnance Survey Landranger, 1:50 000

Sheet Number	Area
86	Haltwhistle and Alston
87	Hexham, Haltwhistle and surrounding area
91	Appleby-in-Westmorland

Ordnance Survey Outdoor Leisure, 1:25 000

Sheet Number	Area
31	Teesdale

YORKSHIRE DALES
Ordnance Survey Pathfinder, 1:25 000

Sheet Number	Area
SD69/79 or 617	Sedbergh and Baugh Fell

Ordnance Survey Landranger, 1:50 000

Sheet Number	Area
91	Appleby-in-Westmorland
97	Kendal to Morecambe
98	Wensleydale and Warfedale

Ordnance Survey Outdoor Leisure, 1:25 000

Sheet Number	Area
2	Yorkshire Dales - Western area
30	Yorkshire Dales - Northern and Central areas

PEAK DISTRICT and DARTMOOR
Ordnance Survey Landranger, 1:50 000

Sheet Number	Area
110	Sheffield and Huddersfield area
191	Okehampton and North Dartmoor area

Ordnance Survey Outdoor Leisure, 1:25 000

Sheet Number	Area
1	The Peak District - Dark Peak area
28	Dartmoor

NORTHERN LAKE DISTRICT
Ordnance Survey Landranger, 1:50 000

Sheet Number	Area
89	West Cumbria
90	Penrith, Keswick and Ambleside area

Ordnance Survey Outdoor Leisure, 1:25 000

Sheet Number	Area
4	The English Lakes - North Western area
5	The English Lakes - North Eastern area

EASTERN LAKE DISTRICT
Ordnance Survey Landranger, 1:50 000

Sheet Number	Area
90	Penrith, Keswick and Ambleside area

Ordnance Survey Outdoor Leisure, 1:25 000

Sheet Number	Area
5	The English Lakes - North Eastern area
7	The English Lakes - South Eastern area

FAR EASTERN LAKE DISTRICT
Ordnance Survey Landranger, 1:50 000

Sheet Number	Area
90	Penrith, Keswick and Ambleside area

Ordnance Survey Outdoor Leisure, 1:25 000

Sheet Number	Area
5	The English Lakes - North Eastern area
7	The English Lakes - South Eastern area

SOUTHERN LAKE DISTRICT
Ordnance Survey Landranger, 1:50 000

Sheet Number	Area
89	West Cumbria
90	Penrith, Keswick and Ambleside area
96	Barrow-in-Furness and South Lakeland area

Ordnance Survey Outdoor Leisure, 1:25 000

Sheet Number	Area
4	The English Lakes - North Western area
6	The English Lakes - South Western area
7	The English Lakes - South Eastern area

WESTERN LAKE DISTRICT
Ordnance Survey Landranger, 1:50 000

Sheet Number	Area
89	West Cumbria
90	Penrith, Keswick and Ambleside area

Ordnance Survey Outdoor Leisure, 1:25 000

Sheet Number	Area
4	The English Lakes - North Western area
6	The English Lakes - South Western area

NORTH WESTERN LAKE DISTRICT
Ordnance Survey Landranger, 1:50 000

Sheet Number	Area
89	West Cumbria
90	Penrith, Keswick and Ambleside area

Ordnance Survey Outdoor Leisure, 1:25 000

Sheet Number	Area
4	The English Lakes - North Western area

CENTRAL LAKE DISTRICT
Ordnance Survey Landranger, 1:50 000

Sheet Number	Area
89	West Cumbria
90	Penrith, Keswick and Ambleside area

Ordnance Survey Outdoor Leisure, 1:25 000

Sheet Number	Area
4	The English Lakes - North Western area
6	The English Lakes - South Western area
7	The English Lakes - South Eastern area

Index

Name	Height in metres	Page

Name	Height in metres	Page
Esk Pike	885	152
Fairfield	873	98
Fellbarrow	416	175
Fell Head	640	48
Fendrith Hill	696	27
Fiend's Fell	634	27
Fleetwith Pike	648	175
Flinty Fell	614	28
Fountains Fell	668	49
Froswick	720	122
Gavel Fell	526	176
Gibson Knott	410	214
Glaramara	783	153
Glenridding Dodd	442	99
Gowbarrow Fell	481	99
Gragareth	627	49
Grange Fell	415	215
Grasmoor	852	199
Gray Crag	699	123
Graystones	456	199
Great Borne	616	176
Great Calva	690	83
Great Carrs	785	154
Great Cockup	526	83
Great Coum	687	50
Great Crag	440	215
Great Dodd	857	100
Great Dun Fell	848	28
Great Gable	899	177
Great Knoutberry Hill	672	50
Great Lingy Hill	616	84
Great Mell Fell	537	100
Great Rigg (inc. Stone Arthur)	766	101
Great Sca Fell	651	84
Great Shunner Fell	716	51
Great Stony Hill	708	29
Great Whernside	704	52
Green Crag	488	156
Green Gable	801	178
Green Hill	628	52
Green Side	795	101
Grey Crag	638	123
Grey Friar	770	156
Grey Knotts	697	179
Grey Nag	656	29
Grike	488	179
Grisedale Pike	791	200

Name	Height in metres	Page
Hallin Fell	388	124
Hangingstone Hill	743	11
Hard Knott	549	157
Harrison Stickle	736	216
Harrop Pike	637	124
Hart Crag	822	102
Harter Fell (F. E. Lake District)	778	125
Harter Fell (S. Lake District)	653	157
Hart Side	756	102
Hartshorn Pike	545	16
Hartsop-above-How	570	103
Hartsop Dodd	618	126
Harwood Common	718	30
Haycock	797	180
Haystacks	597	181
Hedgehope Hill	714	12
Helm Crag	405	217
Helvellyn	950	104/5
Helvellyn Lower Man	925	106
Hen Comb	509	182
Heron Pike	612	107
High Crag	744	182
Higher Shelf Stones	621	69
High Hartsop Dodd	519	107
High Neb	458	70
High Pike (E. Lake District)	656	108
High Pike (N. Lake District)	658	85
High Pike Hill	642	53
High Raise (F. E. Lake District)	802	126
High Raise (C. Lake District)	762	218
High Rigg	350	218
High Seat (C. Lake District)	608	219
High Seat (Yorkshire Dales)	709	53
High Spy	653	200
High Stile	807	183
High Street	828	127
High Tove	515	219
High Willhays	621	74
Hindscarth	727	201
Hobcarton End	634	201
Holme Fell	317	158
Hopegill Head	770	202
Hugh Seat	688	54
Ill Bell	757	128
Ill Crag	935	158
Illgill Head	609	159
Ingleborough	723	55
Iron Crag	640	183

Name	Height in metres	Page
Kentmere Pike	730	128
Kidsty Pike	780	129
Killhope Law	673	30
Kinder Scout	636	71
Kirk Fell	802	184
Knock Fell	794	31
Knott	710	86
Knott Rigg	556	202
Knoutberry Haw	676	56
Knoutberry Hill	668	31
Ladyside Pike	703	203
Lamb Hill	511	12
Lank Rigg	541	185
Latrigg	367	86
Ling Fell	373	203
Lingmell	800	160
Lingmoor Fell	469	160
Little Calva	642	87
Little Dun Fell	842	32
Little Fell (Pennines)	748	32
Little Fell (Yorkshire Dales)	667	56
Little Hart Crag	637	109
Little Mell Fell	505	110
Little Stand	740	161
Loadpot Hill	671	130
Loft Crag	670	220
Longlands Fell	482	87
Long Man Hill	658	33
Long Side	734	88
Lonscale Fell	715	88
Lord's Seat (N. W. Lake District)	552	204
Lord's Seat (Peak District)	550	72
Loughrigg Fell	335	220
Lovely Seat	675	57
Low Fell	423	185
Low Pike	508	110
Low Saddle	656	221
Maiden Moor	670	204
Mam Tor	517	72
Mardale Ill Bell	760	131
Margery Hill	546	73
Meal Fell	540	89
Meldon Hill	767	33
Mellbreak	512	186
Melmerby Fell	709	34
Mickle Fell	788	34
Mid Fell	561	16
Middle Dodd	654	111
Middle Fell	582	186
Middlehope Moor	612	35

Name	Height in metres	Page
Mill Hill	544	73
Mozie Law	552	13
Mungrisdale Common	633	89
Murton Fell	675	35
Nab Scar	445	111
Nethermost Pike	891	112
Nine Standards Rigg	662	57
Outberry Plain	653	36
Outerside	568	205
Pavey Ark	700	221
Peel Fell	602	17
Pen-y-ghent	694	58
Pike of Blisco	705	161
Pike of Stickle	709	222
Pillar	892	187
Place Fell	657	132
Plover Hill	680	58
Raise	883	113
Rampsgill Head	792	133
Randygill Top	624	59
Rannerdale Knotts	355	205
Raven Crag	461	222
Red Pike, Buttermere	755	188
Red Pike, Wasdale	826	189
Red Screes	776	114
Rest Dodd	696	134
Rise Hill	556	59
Robinson	737	206
Rogan's Seat	672	60
Rossett Pike	651	162
Rosthwaite Fell	612	163
Rough Crag	628	135
Round Hill	686	36
Sail	773	206
Sails	666	60
Saint Sunday Crag	841	115
Sale Fell	359	207
Sale How	666	90
Sallows	516	135
Sand Hill	756	207
Scafell	964	164
Scafell Pike	978	165
Scar Crags	672	208
Scaud Hill	694	37
Scoat Fell	841	189
Seatallan	693	190

Name	Height in metres	Page

We publish guides to individual towns, plus books on walking and cycling in the great outdoors throughout England and Wales. This is a recent selection:

Lake District

THE LAKELAND SUMMITS – Tim Synge *(£7.95)*

100 LAKE DISTRICT HILL WALKS – Gordon Brown *(£7.95)*

LAKELAND ROCKY RAMBLES: Geology beneath your feet – Brian Lynas *(£7.95)*

FULL DAYS ON THE LAKELAND FELLS: Challenging Walks – Adrian Dixon *(£7.95)*

STROLLING WITH STEAM : walks along the Keswick Railway – Jan Darrall *(£4.95)*

TEA SHOP WALKS IN THE LAKE DISTRICT – Jean Patefield *(£6.95)*

MOSTLY DOWNHILL: LEISURELY WALKS, LAKE DISTRICT – Alan Pears *(£6.95)*

LAKELAND WALKING, ON THE LEVEL – Norman Buckley *(£6.95)*

PUB WALKS IN THE LAKE DISTRICT – Neil Coates *(£6.95)*

Wales

HILL WALKS IN MID WALES – Dave Ing *(£8.95)*

WELSH WALKS: Dolgellau /Cambrian Coast – L. Main & M. Perrott *(£5.95)*

WELSH WALKS: Aberystwyth & District – L. Main & M. Perrott *(£5.95)*

WALKS IN MYSTERIOUS WALES – Laurence Main *(£7.95)*

RAMBLES IN NORTH WALES – Roger Redfern *(£6.95)*

PUB WALKS IN SNOWDONIA – Laurence Main *(£6.95)*

Peak District, Pennines and Yorkshire

SECRET YORK: WALKS WITHIN THE CITY WALLS – Les Pierce *(£6.95)*

FIFTY CLASSIC WALKS IN THE PENNINES – Terry Marsh *(£8.95)*

PUB WALKS IN THE YORKSHIRE DALES – Clive Price *(£6.95)*

PUB WALKS ON THE NORTH YORK MOORS & COAST – Stephen Rickerby *(£6.95)*

PUB WALKS IN THE YORKSHIRE WOLDS – Tony Whittaker *(£6.95)*

BEST PUB WALKS IN & AROUND SHEFFIELD – Clive Price *(£6.95)*

BEST PUB WALKS IN SOUTH YORKSHIRE – Martin Smith *(£6.95)*

YORKSHIRE DALES WALKING: ON THE LEVEL – Norman Buckley *(£6.95)*

MOSTLY DOWNHILL IN THE PEAK DISTRICT – Clive Price *(£6.95)*
(two volumes, White Peak & Dark Peak)
RAMBLES AROUND MANCHESTER – Mike Cresswell *(£5.95)*
WEST PENNINE WALKS – Mike Cresswell *(£5.95)*

Cycling

CYCLE UK! The essential guide to leisure cycling – Les Lumsdon *(£9.95)*
OFF-BEAT CYCLING IN THE PEAK DISTRICT – Clive Smith *(£6.95)*
MORE OFF-BEAT CYCLING IN THE PEAK DISTRICT – Clive Smith *(£6.95)*
50 BEST CYCLE RIDES IN CHESHIRE – Graham Beech *(£7.95)*
CYCLING IN SCOTLAND & N.E.ENGLAND – Philip Routledge *(£7.95)* .
CYCLING IN NORTH WALES – Philip Routledge *(£7.95) ... available 1996*

Northern England folklore & heritage

SHADOWS: A NORTHERN INVESTIGATION OF THE UNKNOWN – Steve Cliffe *(£7.95)*
DARK TALES OF OLD CHESHIRE – Angela Conway *(£6.95)*
CHESHIRE: ITS MAGIC & MYSTERY – Doug Pickford *(£7.95)*
GHOSTS, TRADITIONS & LEGENDS OF LANCASHIRE – Ken Howarth *(£7.95)*
JOURNEY THROUGH LANCASHIRE – Kenneth Fields *(£7.95)*
OLD NOTTINGHAMSHIRE REMEMBERED – Keith Taylor *(£7.95)*
STRANGE SOUTH YORKSHIRE – David Clarke *(£6.95)*
TRADITIONAL PUBS OF OLD LANCASHIRE – Peter Barnes *(£7.95)*

Sport

RED FEVER: from Rochdale to Rio as 'United' supporters – Steve Donoghue *(£7.95)*
UNITED WE STOOD: unofficial history of the Ferguson years – Richard Kurt *(£6.95)*
MANCHESTER CITY: Moments to Remember – John Creighton *(£9.95)*

- plus many more entertaining and educational books being regularly added to our list.
All of our books are available from your local bookshop. In case of difficulty, or to obtain our complete catalogue, please contact:

Sigma Leisure, 1 South Oak Lane, Wilmslow, Cheshire SK9 6AR
Phone: 01625 – 531035   Fax: 01625 – 536800

ACCESS and VISA orders welcome – call our friendly sales staff or use our 24 hour Answerphone service! Most orders are despatched on the day we receive your order – you could be enjoying our books in just a couple of days. Please add £2 p&p to all orders.